HOW TO WRITE

Research Papers

3rd edition

Sharon Sorenson

THOMSON

ARCO

Australia • Canada • Mexico • Singapore • Spain • United Kingdom • United States

THOMSON
ARCO ™

An ARCO Book

ARCO is a registered trademark of Thomson Learning, Inc., and is used herein under license by Peterson's.

About The Thomson Corporation and Peterson's

With revenues of US$7.2 billion, The Thomson Corporation (www.thomson.com) is a leading global provider of integrated information solutions for business, education, and professional customers. Its Learning businesses and brands (www.thomson. rning com) serve the needs of individuals, learning institutions, and corporations with products and services for both traditional and distributed learning.

Peterson's, part of The Thomson Corporation, is one of the nation's most respected providers of lifelong learning online resources, software, reference guides, and books. The Education Supersite[SM] at www.petersons.com—the Internet's most heavily traveled education resource—has searchable databases and interactive tools for contacting U.S.-accredited institutions and programs. In addition, Peterson's serves more than 105 million education consumers annually.

For more information, contact Peterson's, 2000 Lenox Drive, Lawrenceville, NJ 08648; 800-338-3282; or find us on the World Wide Web at www.petersons.com/about.

Third Edition

ISBN 0-7689-0925-2

Printed in Canada

10 9 8 7 6 5 4 3   04 03 02

Contents

Chapter One: Defining the Research Paper   1

Chapter Two: Developing the Subject   3
    Step 1: Prewriting—Planning Your Time   3
    Step 2: Prewriting—Selecting A Suitable Subject   5
    Step 3: Prewriting—Writing A Tentative Thesis Sentence   10

Chapter Three: Finding Secondary Resources   13
    Step 4: Prewriting—Developing A Preliminary Bibliography   13
    Step 5: Prewriting—Shaping The Preliminary Outline   18

Chapter Four: Using the Secondary Resources   21
    Step 6: Prewriting—Taking Notes   21
    Step 7: Prewriting—Writing Precis And Paraphrases   27

Chapter Five: Using Primary Research   31
    Step 8: Prewriting—Conducting Primary Research   31

Chapter Six: Drafting the Paper   33
    Step 9: Writing—Creating The Final Plan   33
    Step 10: Writing—Developing The First Draft   37
    Step 11: Revising—Polishing The Content   41

Chapter Seven: Preparing the Documentation   47
    Step 12: Revising—Preparing Final Documentation Notes   48
    Step 13: Revising—Preparing The Final Bibliography   49

Chapter Eight: Preparing the Final Copy   61
   Step 14: Revising—Formatting The Final Draft   61
   Step 15: Proofreading—Checking The Details   64

Chapter Nine: Studying the Models   67
   MLA Parenthetical Style Sample   79
   Endnote Style   80
   Footnote Style   84
   APA Style   88
   Numbered Bibliography Style   96

Chapter One

Defining the Research Paper

A research paper, sometimes called a term paper or library paper, reports the writer's research findings. Literally, a research paper involves "searching again" through what others have written about the subject. In reality, however, a research paper may take one of two approaches: It may be a summary of information from many resources, or it may be an evaluation of research information.

If the paper summarizes research, you tell only about what you read, and the reading may be from a single source or, more likely, from many sources. On the other hand, if the paper evaluates the research information, it considers *why* or *how* and is frequently either a comparison-contrast paper or a cause-effect paper. The evaluation paper requires the use of numerous sources and assumes the writer's ability to show originality and imagination.

Chances are, your teacher will clarify what kind of research paper you are to write. For instance, if the teacher assigns a paper that is to explore the importance of wetlands in waterfowl migration, you will summarize what authoritative resources say about the topic. If, on the other hand, your teacher assigns a paper that is to compare two short stories, two battles, or two scientific theories, it is unlikely that you will find such comparisons already published. Thus, you will read what authorities have written about the respective stories, battles, or theories and then write a paper that demonstrates your own conclusions about similarities and/or differences.

In the first instance, with the wetlands paper, you are merely reporting what others have already said. In the second instance, with the comparisons, you are evaluating what others have said in order to develop your own thesis.

In some cases, however, your teacher may simply assign "a research paper," allowing you considerable freedom to choose the topic and the kind of paper you will write based on personal interest. More on that later.

First, let's take a look at what makes a research paper.

CHARACTERISTICS

An effective research paper fulfills these requirements:

- indicates careful, comprehensive reading and understanding of the topic
- establishes, in its introduction, a thesis to be developed in the course of the paper
- is clearly organized
- employs the principles of good composition
- includes direct quotations, paraphrases, or precis that support the thesis
- includes documentation in the form of parenthetical notes, endnotes, or footnotes
- includes a list of works cited
- exhibits careful, thorough documentation of sources of ideas
- follows a carefully prescribed format
- is always typed and printed on a letter-quality printer.

PROCESS

The step-by-step process of developing a research paper seems rather direct as it is spelled out in this book. Be aware, however, that the research process always requires a kind of "yo-yo" approach.

The Yo-Yo Approach Defined

Rather than completing one step of the research/writing process and moving neatly on to the next step, you will find that you confront problems that cause you either to go back to a previous step or to think ahead to the next step.

For instance, just when you think that you have completed all the necessary research, you may discover that you need new information to fill a gap or to add support. Or just when you think you have completed a sensible outline, you may find that the paper does not flow smoothly given its method of organization. So you go back—rethink, reread, rewrite. The yo-yo process continues until you have finished proofreading your final draft.

The steps in this book show you how to develop an effective research paper. The process works well, especially if you understand—and accept as a fact of the research life—the yo-yo approach.

Chapter Two

Developing the Subject

Chances are your instructor will have assigned a paper of a certain length due on a specific date. Perhaps you have a general topic. Given these parameters, you must select a narrowed topic, research it, and prepare a final paper. So let's get started.

STEP 1: **PREWRITING—** PLANNING YOUR TIME

One of the hardest parts of writing a research paper is planning your time so that you don't find yourself working all night just before the paper is due. Students often do not realize how much time the library search involves, how much time the reading and note-taking require, how much time the drafting process entails, and, above all, how much time careful revision demands. The students who type all night to have a paper ready for an 8 A.M. class hand in a first draft. By omitting the revision process, they omit any chances of having a good paper. But, we are getting ahead of ourselves.

To begin, make a plan. Use the following guidelines, recognizing that a week represents five working days. You choose the days.

If your final draft is due in **10 weeks**, spend

> 4 days choosing a topic (Step 2)
> 6 days doing preliminary work (Steps 3, 4, and 5)
> 12 days taking notes (Steps 6 and 7)
> 7 days seeking primary references (Step 8)
> 1 day developing the final outline (Step 9)
> 9 days writing a first draft (Step 10)
> 4 days revising (Step 11)
> 6 days documenting and polishing (Steps 12, 13, and 14)
> 1 day proofreading (Step 15)

If your final draft is due in **8 weeks**, spend

> 3 days choosing a topic (Step 2)
> 5 days doing preliminary work (Steps 3, 4, and 5)
> 10 days taking notes (Steps 6 and 7)
> 5 days seeking primary references (Step 8)
> 1 day developing the final outline (Step 9)
> 7 days writing a first draft (Step 10)
> 3 days revising (Step 11)
> 5 days documenting and polishing (Steps 12, 13, and 14)
> 1 day proofreading (Step 15)

If your paper is due in **6 weeks**, spend

> 2 days choosing a topic (Step 2)
> 4 days doing preliminary work (Steps 3, 4, and 5)
> 8 days taking notes (Steps 6 and 7)
> 3 days seeking primary references (Step 8)
> 1 day developing the final outline (Step 9)
> 5 days writing a first draft (Step 10)
> 2 days revising (Step 11)
> 4 days documenting and polishing (Steps 12, 13, and 14)
> 1 day proofreading (Step 15)

If your paper is due in **4 weeks**, spend

> 1 day choosing a topic (Step 2)
> 2 days doing preliminary work (Steps 3, 4, and 5)
> 6 days taking notes (Steps 6 and 7)
> 2 days seeking primary references (Step 8)
> 1 day developing the final outline (Step 9)
> 3 days writing a first draft (Step 10)
> 1 day revising (Step 11)
> 3 days documenting and polishing (Steps 12, 13, and 14)
> 1 day proofreading (Step 15)

Mark a calendar now to remind yourself at what point you should have each step completed. Then make sure you stick to the schedule.

STEP 2: **PREWRITING—**
SELECTING A SUITABLE SUBJECT

With your time line in place, let's get to work. Your next task is to select a suitable subject. "Suitable" depends on four factors:

1. length of time you have to research and develop your paper
Do you have two weeks or two months?

2. length of paper
Is it to be 1,000 words or 5,000 words?

3. availability of secondary resources
Does your school or local library have the necessary materials or must you request information by mail or through an interlibrary loan? Are computer databases available with immediate access?

4. need for primary research
Will interviews, surveys, experiments, or data analyses be necessary?

Your choice of subject can make or break your paper. If you choose a subject of little or no interest to you, you'll have trouble sticking to the task. If you tackle a subject too broad, you'll never be able to develop and successfully support your thesis. If you select a subject too narrow, you won't find enough material to flesh out the paper. So selecting the right subject may very well determine your chances of success.

In some cases, you may be assigned a broad research topic; in other cases, you may be free to select whatever topic you wish. For instance, if your instructor assigns a paper that "addresses some major idea we've studied in this course," your general topic is assigned. You must narrow it.

If, on the other hand, your instructor assigns a paper that "demonstrates your understanding of the research process," the general topic is yours for the choosing. In that case, where do you turn for general topics? Consider the following sources:

Personal Interests

Personal interests might include hobbies, favorite courses, part-time jobs, and career plans.

These can also lead to behind-the-scenes ideas. For instance, if your hobby is computer games, you may wonder about how they are designed, developed, packaged, protected, marketed, or used. But your interest may also lead you to think about board games or card games, or games in other cultures, perhaps exploring those from your own cultural heritage. If you hold a part-time job at a fast-food chain, you may want to investigate how franchises work, how managers are trained, or how products are advertised. But your interest may also lead you to think about nutrition, food processing, additives and preservatives, packaging, or recycling.

Daily Media

Daily media outlets include television, radio, newspapers, and news magazines.

Granted, a topic too new will have too little information available for your research. Thus, listen for ideas *behind* the news stories. An item about a high-profile murder may lead you to questions about the media coverage, judicial system, prison system, use of technology in the courtroom, or even other countries' treatment of murderers. Likewise, listen to what others such as, family, neighbors, teachers, pastors, and news commentators say about the news.

General School Work

Included in this source are classes and extracurricular activities.

If your favorite class is science, consider a topic related to your coursework: What creates autumn colors or brilliant sunsets? What caused the hole in the ozone? What happens to patients in the course of Alzheimer's disease? Why is the Alyeska pipeline a technological phenomenon?

Most important in searching for an appropriate topic is to maintain an active, curious mind. When you do, you'll find general topics all around you. Pick one that interests you: You'll be spending many hours with it!

Your next task is to find a way to do something manageable with your broad, general topic.

In order to narrow the general topic and to determine the purpose of the paper, you should do exploratory reading in the general area. Browse through encyclopedias, magazines, reference books, and CD-ROMs and electronic bulletin boards for thought-provoking ideas that will help you think of an appropriate way to narrow the subject. Read quickly, letting your mind work freely.

Technology Notes

Many libraries have reference materials on CD-ROM. Most of these programs have easy-to-use, pull-down menus that give you on-screen, step-by-step help, so you don't have to be afraid to use them. Some provide full-text articles and others only provide summaries, but all represent a variety of respected periodicals. You can access these articles via several means. Title search—referred to as "title browse" in some programs—is especially helpful. You may find, for example, categories such as aging, alcohol, communication, consumerism, economics, ethics, family, food, government, habitat, health, human rights, life science, money, physical science, population, technology, transportation, work, and youth. By browsing through titles found under these topics, you may find not only an interesting topic, but also a way to narrow a broad one.

Also consult electronic bulletin boards or other computer network information sources. People with interests similar to yours will probably offer ideas, suggest secondary sources, or provide primary research.

Once you have a general idea for a topic, put it in the form of a question. Answers to this question will suggest narrowed topics, some of them possibly suitable for your research paper.

Let's follow Alicia as she narrows her general topic. (Note: Alicia's complete paper appears in Chapter Nine.) For personal reasons she wants to investigate some aspect of Alzheimer's disease. Last summer she worked as a volunteer on the Alzheimer's wing of a nursing home; now her widowed grandfather suffers from the disease and has moved in with her family. To narrow the very broad topic of Alzheimer's disease, Alicia formulated a question and then tried to answer it:

General topic: What does she need to know in order to understand Alzheimer's disease?

By browsing through some pamphlets from the library's vertical file, Alicia found the following answers. These answers suggest potential narrowed topics:

Narrowed topics: symptoms—physical, mental

diagnosis—if? when? how?

causes

treatment—early, later

patient support—what? how?

family support

> types of care for patients
>
> nursing homes—if? when?
>
> finances, insurance
>
> activities for patients

Alicia next checked the library's computer catalog and picked two books on the general topic of Alzheimer's disease. She skimmed the books by looking first at the tables of contents and then reading the first and last sentences of paragraphs in two or three key chapters. In her exploratory reading, she discovered that most of her so-called narrowed topics were still quite broad. For instance, in her quick look in the computer catalog, she found whole books on home care of Alzheimer's patients—an indication that she was not finished with the narrowing process.

One evening as she watched a television documentary about Alzheimer's, Alicia heard words that caught her immediate attention. The documentary's host said that when an Alzheimer's patient moves in with the family and finds him- or herself in the same house with a teenager, frustration levels go up. The teen, seeking her own adult identity, runs head-on into a grandparent losing his/hers.

Alicia knew she had found the narrowed topic she wanted. She worded her narrowed topic as another question:

Suitable subject: How can a teenager cope with having an Alzheimer's patient in the house?

Use the same process to narrow your own broad subject to something manageable:

1. Word your general topic as a question.

2. Browse through an encyclopedia, the vertical file, a CD-ROM program, or some other general reference, reading about your general topic.

3. Answer your general-topic question, creating a list of narrowed topics.

4. Skim one or two general books or lengthy articles on your topic.

5. Keep an active mind as you strive to narrow your topic.

6. Word your narrowed topic as a question.

POSSIBLE PITFALLS

Selecting a suitable subject is so vital that a few warnings are in order. Be critical enough to evaluate your proposed subject according to these possible pitfalls:

The subject may be too broad.

Even though you may have been asked to write a 1,500-word paper, keep in mind what this word count represents: A five-paragraph theme may be well over 700 words, and magazine articles often run no more than 3,000 words. So don't try to cope with a book-length subject in half the length of a magazine article.

The subject may be too limited for research.

Two kinds of topics may end up being too limited. In one case, if little or no research material is available, you cannot write a successful research paper (maybe the subject is too new). Or, in another case, if the subject lacks depth, you cannot write a successful paper. For example, every book you consult will explain in the same way the process for making paper in your own kitchen; thus the topic is unsuitable for a research paper.

The subject may be too technical.

Unless you already have a good background in computer technology, for instance, you should not attempt to write a paper explaining how a computer works. Unless a paper is part of an assignment for a technical class, avoid subjects which rely heavily on technical terms.

The subject may be too ordinary.

Research should provide new information, or at least a new way of looking at old information. To try to do research on the effects of sunscreen lotion on skin exposed to ultraviolet rays will probably prove tiresome and dull—unless, of course, you have just invented a revolutionary sunscreen lotion.

The subject may be too controversial.

A highly contested issue may prove to be more than a single, carefully organized research paper can describe or evaluate. If volumes have already been written about your narrowed topic, chances are you have not chosen well.

Avoiding these kinds of pitfalls will help you select a workable, satisfactory subject.

STEP 3: **PREWRITING—** WRITING A TENTATIVE THESIS SENTENCE

Once you have narrowed the subject, apply your logic and imagination to determine what your paper should include. Make a list of the possible topics to cover. To help you think through the list, put yourself in the reader's seat. What do you want to know about this subject? What questions need answers? Let's check with Alicia again for an example.

Suitable subject: Teenagers Coping with Alzheimer's Patients

Possible subtopics: Alzheimer's symptoms

disease progression

patient's behavior

patient's emotions

home care

caregiver's problems

other family members' concerns

patient frustration

family frustration

sources of patient/family frustration

reducing everyone's frustration

treatments

daily routine

communication with patient

nutrition

support groups for family

support groups for teens

day care

nursing home—if? when?

teen's social life

teen's school life (homework,
    extracurricular activities)

Alicia knows her list is too long, but she doesn't know how much information she will find on some of these subtopics. On the other hand, her list now includes specific details as opposed to the broad topics in her earlier list. This list of subtopics will guide her research.

By developing your own list of subtopics at the start, you prevent a significant waste of time later. Most importantly, you will avoid reading unrelated material. Of course, a preliminary list is just that—preliminary. It will change as you do your research. So, develop a list of possible subtopics to guide your early research.

Technology Note

Numerous software programs offer prewriting activities to help you think through your topic, organize ideas, and consider imaginative approaches. You may find one or more of these programs beneficial at this step.

Now that you have narrowed the topic and developed a list, you are ready to write a tentative thesis statement. A thesis statement has two primary characteristics: it states or suggests the paper's main topics and it states or implies the order in which the ideas will appear. In other words, the subtopic appearing first in the thesis sentence appears in the first paragraph.

How do you formulate a thesis sentence from your list of subtopics? Alicia studied her list and sorted the items into two broad categories. Her reasoning went something like this:

- *Patient's emotions* are probably the result of Alzheimer's symptoms and the disease's *progression*.

- The *emotions* affect the patient's *behavior*.

- *Frustration* probably best describes the *emotion*.

- So *patient's emotions* should be one main idea.

- If a *patient's emotions* form one main idea, then it's logical that *family emotions* make up another main idea.

- That topic includes the ideas of *caregiver's problems, family members' concerns, family frustration, decisions about a nursing home, teen's school and social life.*

- **The remaining ideas fit loosely into the category of** *reducing frustrations*—**either those of the patient or of the family.**

  With that logic, Alicia formulated the following preliminary thesis:

  Suitable subject: Teenagers Coping with Alzheimer's Patients

  Thesis Statement: Understanding the emotions of both the
                                patient and the family will help reduce
                                everyone's frustrations.

  **Main points
  (in implied order):**   patient's emotions
                                family members' emotions
                                reduction of patient's frustrations
                                reduction of family members' frustrations

Like the preliminary list you prepared earlier, your thesis statement may change somewhat. (See Alicia's model paper in Chapter Nine to compare the preliminary thesis statement with the final one.) Nevertheless, the preliminary thesis will serve as a guide throughout your research.

So, write one now.

Chapter Three

Finding Secondary Resources

Armed with a sense of direction and a tentative thesis statement, you are ready to do serious library work. So, the next step is to develop a preliminary bibliography.

STEP 4: **PREWRITING—**
DEVELOPING A PRELIMINARY BIBLIOGRAPHY

The bibliography is an alphabetical list of the sources used in developing a research paper. The best way to prepare this list is to prepare a bibliography card for each source as you find it. These cards comprise your preliminary bibliography. Indeed, you will no doubt find sources that at first seem promising but that in the end you do not use; you will simply eliminate these cards. Ultimately, it will be only a matter of alphabetizing the cards and typing their information, and, your bibliography will be finished.

Now that you have a thesis and a list of possible topics to explore within the confines of your narrowed subject, you will need to select books, magazines, pamphlets, and other print and nonprint sources that seem to include pertinent information. Go to the library and consult the card catalog or computer catalog, the *Reader's Guide to Periodical Literature*, the vertical file, and the various reference books available. As you search, check under more than one heading. You may need to think of synonyms, broader or narrower categories, or other related words.

Technology Notes

Most libraries have computer catalogs that allow you several means by which to search:

- subject search
- word search
- author search
- title search

If your topic is too broad, you may also need to restrict your subject search. For instance, when Alicia asked for the subject "Alzheimer's," she found 96 entries—too many to skim. A word search found 47 entries—still too many. Next she added a restrictor and asked for "Alzheimer's" and "families." That produced a manageable list of 21 entries.

Also, CD-ROM reference materials usually include subject and keyword searches similar to those in computer catalogs. Often you can also add restrictors to these searches. When Alicia asked for "Alzheimer's," she found 756 articles; but when she added restrictors, she had very different results. "Alzheimer's" along with "teenagers" produced zero listings, but "Alzheimer's" along with "caregivers" gave her 25 listings. These she could skim quickly on screen.

Some CD-ROM reference materials include only summaries. They, too, significantly speed your search. No longer must you find the magazine (or the microfilm or microfiche), find the specific article, and skim it only to discover it has nothing helpful. Instead, you can skim the summary on screen and then know whether or not to include the source in your preliminary bibliography.

In addition to these sources, a few others are worth mentioning. If your topic is current, NewsBank (a microfiche file of contemporary topics from widely circulated United States newspapers) is one good source. When Alicia looked in the index under "Alzheimer's," she found numerous subtopics like "care facilities," "detection," "prevention," "research," and "treatment." Only the section on "care facilities" and "research" had information pertinent to her thesis. But what a quick, easy way to find current newspaper articles from across the United States!

Depending on your topic, another general reference you may want to check is *Facts on File: Weekly World News Digest.* When Alicia checked "Alzheimer's Disease," she found a cross-reference that said, "See under Medicine and Health."

Among the six entries she found for that year were also cross-references to additional articles.

As you find materials that seem useful, prepare bibliography cards for those books, magazines, and other sources. Prepare a separate 3″ × 5″ card for each source. Using this approach, you can get rid of cards for sources that later prove useless. Similarly, you can alphabetize those that prove helpful. Write in ink—pencil will smear and become illegible as you handle the cards. Follow these general instructions for making bibliography cards:

For books:

- List the call number in the upper left corner.
- List the author, last name first.
  If there is an editor instead, list his or her name, followed by *ed*.

  If there are two authors, list the name of the first author in reverse order but list the name of the second author in natural order.

  If there are more than two authors, list the name of the first author in reverse order and follow it with *and others*.

- Write the title and underline it.
- Give the publication information: city of publication, publisher, and year of publication.
- Add any notes from the card or computer catalog that may be helpful in your later search (bibliography, illustrations, number of pages, etc.).
- If you use more than one library, note on the bottom line of the card the library in which you found this source.
- Number the card in the upper right corner. Begin with 1 and number sequentially. Later, the numbers will help to quickly identify sources.
  (See Step 13, later, for a comprehensive list of sample bibliography entries.)

For a book, then, a bibliography card will look something like this:

For a magazine, newspaper, or encyclopedia article:

- List the author, if there is one, last name first.
- List the title of the article and enclose it in quotation marks.
- List and underline the name of the magazine, newspaper, or encyclopedia.
- Include, for magazines, the volume number, page numbers, and date.
- Include, for newspapers, the section number and page numbers, and date.
- Include, for encyclopedias, the year of publication.
- Add any notes that may be helpful in locating or using the source.
- Number the card in the upper right corner.

A sample bibliography card for a magazine will look like this:

```
Wilson, H. S.                                    21
"Family Caregiving for a Relative with
Alzheimer's Dementia: Coping with Negative
Choices."
Nursing Research.
38: 94-8, Mar.-Apr. 1989.
```

As you work with the preliminary bibliography, you can begin to decide which books will be of value and which will not. Before you cart home stacks of books and periodicals, check quickly for their apparent usefulness. For instance, in books look at the tables of contents, indexes, and any bibliographies. If nothing suggests information related to your topic, leave those books at the library.

On the other hand, since you will be working primarily with nonfiction books, which are arranged on the library shelf by subject, look through books located near the ones you have selected from the card or computer catalog. Perhaps one of them will be helpful. For instance, when Alicia finished her computer catalog search, she noticed that several titles had call numbers of 618.976 and 362.196. As she pulled those books from the shelf, she scanned nearby titles and found other books that seemed useful. A quick check of the tables of contents and/or indexes helped her decide whether or not to check out the books.

Technology Note

Some computer catalogs permit you to do a call-number search. You can accomplish nearly the same results with this technique.

Likewise, as you search through the *Reader's Guide* and other periodical indexes, think of alternate headings under which you may find sources. Sometimes the headings that appear in the guide are not the same ones you might think of first. And do not hesitate to ask the reference librarian for suggested *Reader's Guide* headings suitable for your topic.

Technology Note

For particularly obscure topics, you may wish to do a computer search that will tell you what information is available in computer-linked libraries all over the United States. This information is available through interlibrary loan. Check with your librarian for details.

STEP 5: **PREWRITING—** SHAPING THE PRELIMINARY OUTLINE

The next step is to develop an outline from the list and tentative thesis sentence you wrote in Step 3 (page 13). By now, as a result of your work with the preliminary bibliography, you have done additional skimming. You may be ready to think through the organization of ideas. If not, read a couple of general articles about your subject. If an encyclopedia includes an article about your subject, begin there. Then, once you have done some general reading and skimming, develop an outline.

While your first reaction may be to skip the preliminary outline, don't! Your argument may be the typical one: How can I develop an outline when I have not read all the materials available?

The answer comes in the form of another question: How do you know which materials to read if you have not determined what your paper ought to do? In other words, developing a preliminary outline now guides your reading in the future, saving hours of reading and avoiding stacks of useless notes.

So, do the outline now.

Using a list like the example in Step 3 above, you could develop a preliminary outline that looks something like Alicia's:

I. Understanding the patient's emotions
    A. Symptoms of disease
    B. Progression of disease
    C. Behavior of patient
II. Reducing patient's frustration
III. Understanding the family's emotions
    A. Caregivers
    B. Teens
IV. Reducing family frustration

As you study Alicia's outline, you will notice that she has no subdivisions under parts II and IV. At this point, she knows too little about how to reduce frustration to include any subdivisions. This preliminary outline, however, helps her focus on her specific research needs.

Whether or not your instructor requires a formal outline, consider these guidelines about the logic of outlining:

- An outline does not reflect a paper's introduction or conclusion.
- In general, each division of the outline represents a fully developed paragraph in the paper. For instance, in Alicia's outline, the first Roman numeral will be her second paragraph, immediately after her introduction. Items A and B may be subtopics in this paragraph. Or A may represent Alicia's second paragraph, and, B the third.
- A good outline reflects the logic of development, so that the summary of the parts of any one subdivision equals the topic of that division. For instance, Alicia's topics A, B, and C together equal part I.
- Every level of the outline will have at least two divisions (you cannot divide anything into fewer than two!), so an item designated *1* will be followed by *2* and an item designated *a* will be followed by *b*.
- The divisions of a logical outline are mutually exclusive. For instance, if you divide *college students* into *male*, *female*, and *nontraditional*, you then have a problem with mutual exclusion. Nontraditional students, those older than most, are either male or female. The divisions overlap. To solve the problem, divide *college students* into *traditional* and *nontraditional*. These two subdivisions could in turn be divided into *male* and *female*. Then each division is mutually exclusive.

Remember, your final outline may be quite different from your preliminary one. You will no doubt choose to make changes, not only in content, but perhaps in organization. This is part of the yo-yo approach.

Chapter Four

Using the Secondary Resources

You have searched the library for books, periodicals, pamphlets, and computer resources. You have stacks of materials. Hidden in all these pages is the information you need to write your research paper.

STEP 6: **PREWRITING**—TAKING NOTES

Now that you have a preliminary bibliography and a preliminary outline, you are ready to begin reading seriously and taking notes. Remember, your reading will be guided by your outline, and your outline can be changed as you proceed.

Because you used 3″ × 5″ cards for your bibliography, you may wish to use 4″ × 6″ cards for your notes. The larger cards hold more and allow for easier reading; but above all, they cannot be accidentally mixed with the bibliography cards.

POSSIBLE PITFALL

Avoid the temptation to fill each card. Regardless of the size, you will put only one idea from one source on a card. Why? Because, once you are ready to write your paper, you will arrange the cards in the order in which you will use their respective bits of information. If more than one idea appears on a card, it will be useless in helping you arrange your ideas. If a card reflects more than one source, you will be unable to document its contents accurately.

Technology Note

Even if you generate note cards at the computer, be sure to follow the guidelines below. In addition, avoid the temptation to enter long passages of text verbatim. To do so will cause you to work harder when you draft your paper.

Use the following guidelines for taking notes.

- Write the number of the bibliography card in the upper right corner of the note card. You will need this information later for documenting your paper. Remember that inaccurate or incomplete documentation is a serious shortcoming. Early and ongoing precautions significantly decrease the potential for error. So be sure to list the source number on *every* note card.
- Alongside the bibliography card number, list the page numbers from which you are about to take notes. This information, too, will be essential for your documentation. Take the time to be accurate and complete with your note cards; this effort will reduce the potential for error in your paper.
- Write the subject, called the *slug*, on the top line of the note card. The slug may be taken from your outline or it may later become an outline topic. Do not use Roman numerals, letters, and numbers from your outline, however, as they may well change, confusing your references. By using a slug, you can later organize your cards by stacking together all those with identical slugs.
- Use a separate note card for each idea from each source. Then, when you organize your note cards, each card will support only one topic.
- Take notes in your own words. You may use phrases, lists, key words, sentences, or paragraphs. Writing precis and paraphrases is so important that you should study the examples in Step 7 on page 32.
- When you find a particularly poignant passage—perhaps a phrase or even a whole sentence or two—then copy it on your note card *exactly* as it appears, comma for comma, letter for letter. Enclose the passage in quotation marks.
- If a word is misspelled or misused in the quoted passage, clarify your accuracy in quoting by inserting the word *sic* (meaning *thus*, to clarify that the error is not yours), in italics (underlined, because it is a foreign word), and enclosed in brackets.

Example:

> **"The recipient hereby expresses his hartfelt [*sic*] thanks for the commendation."**

- If you omit words or phrases or choose not to quote a complete sentence, show the omission by using ellipsis points. Use three points for the omission of a word or phrase; use a fourth point to represent a period at the end of a sentence.

Full text quoted:

> **"You can reinforce your verbal message with nonverbal ones by pointing, gesturing, and using 'body language' to convey your pleasure or displeasure with your relative's behavior."**

Partial text quoted; three ellipses points:

> **"You can reinforce your verbal message with nonverbal ones to convey your pleasure or displeasure with your relative's behavior."**

Partial text quoted; four ellipses points:

> **"You can reinforce your verbal message with nonverbal ones by pointing, gesturing, and using 'body language' to convey your pleasure or displeasure"**

- Use brackets to enclose words you add to quoted material
    —to clarify
    —to refine style.

Example to clarify:

> **"You can reinforce your verbal message with nonverbal ones by pointing, gesturing, and using 'body language' to convey your [reactions to] your relative's behavior."**

Example to refine style:

> **"[One] can reinforce [one's] verbal message with nonverbal ones by pointing, gesturing, and using 'body language' to convey [one's] pleasure or displeasure with [a] relative's behavior."**

- Use single quotation marks inside double quotation marks to set apart words, phrases, or clauses quoted within the passage you are quoting. See the examples immediately above.

Warning:

If you carelessly omit the quotation marks around words not your own, you are in essence stealing. The act is called *plagiarism*, and it is such a serious error that some instructors will automatically fail a paper that neglects to acknowledge sources accurately. So, quote accurately and document accurately.

- As you take notes, revise your preliminary outline as necessary. You will no doubt add subpoints, maybe even main points. Perhaps you will want to change the organization or rethink relationships between topics. Study Alicia's revised outline below. Compare it with her first outline on page 23. Then compare it with her final outline on page 41. Be comfortable with the idea that the outline is a *working* outline; it will continue to change as you complete your research. That, remember, is the yo-yo process.

   I. Understanding one's own emotions
  II. Understanding the patient's emotions
     A. Cognitive effects
       1. Characteristics of the disease
       2. Response to the characteristics
     B. Communication impairments
       1. Characteristics of the disease
       2. Response to the characteristics
     C. Behavior problems
       1. Characteristics of the disease
       2. Response to the characteristics
  III. Dealing with the patient
     A. At home
     B. At nursing home
  IV. Understanding parents
   V. Getting help

    Notice that, at this point in her research, Alicia has filled in details about understanding the patient's emotions, but she has not yet found adequate information for other main divisions in her outline. Your outline will probably follow a similar pattern of change.

- You may need to find additional sources if gaps appear in the outline or if you have no note cards for certain sections of the outline.

In general, you will take three different kinds of notes:

1. Some note cards will have nothing more than phrases, lists, or series of incomplete sentences.

2. Other note cards will combine paraphrases with direct quotations.

3. Still other note cards will record only a pithy direct quotation.

Each is illustrated below.

Caregiver's emotions   5-V-VI

anger, shame, self-pity, guilt,
anxiety, depression, stress

Behavior response — exercise   1-59

Some patients who exercise "seem to be
calmer and do less agitated pacing.... Motor
skills seem to be retained longer if they
are used regularly."

patients involved
sleep at night
walking excellent

```
┌─────────────────────────────────────────────────────────┐
│                                                           │
│  Behavior response - model              7-146            │
│  ─────────────────────────────────────────────────────   │
│   "Think about how you like to be treated,               │
│   and what it must be like to be in the                  │
│   position of the patient."                              │
│  ─────────────────────────────────────────────────────   │
│  ─────────────────────────────────────────────────────   │
│  ─────────────────────────────────────────────────────   │
│  ─────────────────────────────────────────────────────   │
│  ─────────────────────────────────────────────────────   │
│  ─────────────────────────────────────────────────────   │
│  ─────────────────────────────────────────────────────   │
│  ─────────────────────────────────────────────────────   │
│                                                           │
└─────────────────────────────────────────────────────────┘
```

Note the following details about these three samples:

The first card, from bibliography source 5 on pages V–VI, is just a list of words and the slug, "Caregiver's emotions," which comes from the preliminary outline. (See Step 5 on page 22.)

The second card, from bibliography source 1 on page 59, includes a direct quotation combined with paraphrase. Note the use of quotation marks and the ellipses points. Note, too, the acceptable use of incomplete sentences. Again, the slug, "Behavior response," comes from the preliminary outline.

The third note card is a direct quotation. The slug includes the additional notation, "model," to suggest placement among other note cards with the same slug.

POSSIBLE PITFALLS

As you take notes, try to avoid these potential trouble spots:

- Do not rely too heavily on one source. In general, you should have about an equal number of note cards from each source. While it is not uncommon to find one source meeting many of your needs, your paper will be seriously weak from lack of broad research if you limit the variety of sources. This is, after all, a research project, not a book report.

- If your subject permits, try to use book and periodical references equally. To rely too heavily on books will date your paper. To rely too heavily on periodicals may result in cursory research, especially for a topic more thoroughly discussed in book-length sources. Of course, the topic ultimately determines the appropriate sources.
- Be sure to check nonprint media sources, which can provide additional perspectives. Television documentaries, public-radio talk shows, films, lectures— all are legitimate research sources. (See also Step 8: Conducting Primary Research, on page 37.)
- If your subject is controversial, consult equally the sources supporting each side. If your paper is persuasive, you must answer arguments from the "other" side. If your paper is comparison-contrast, you must present both sides.
- Do not overuse direct quotations. You can usually summarize ideas in fewer words. Probably less than one-fourth of your cards should quote directly.
- Make absolutely certain that you have put quotation marks around any words not your own.
- Make absolutely certain that you have listed the bibliography card number and the page number(s) on *each* note card.
- Be sure to include only one idea from one source on each note card.

STEP 7: **PREWRITING**— WRITING PRECIS AND PARAPHRASES

Both the paraphrase and the precis are a kind of summary. The obvious purpose of a summary is to provide a shortened version of a piece of writing, but it can also serve to simplify, to make a passage more reader-friendly. The majority of your notes will be either in paraphrase or precis form, the precis being the shorter summary. Let's look at each.

Paraphrase

A paraphrase restates a passage in your own words. In one sense, it is a summary, because you may be "translating" technical or complicated material into your own vocabulary. In another sense, however, it is not a summary, because it is usually the same length, or nearly the same length, as the original.

A good paraphrase usually

- reflects your own words, your own style of writing
- reduces the original only slightly, usually by less than one-fourth

- displays careful reading of the original
- represents the original idea accurately and completely, without reflecting personal bias
- uses clear, effective sentences as well as good mechanics, usage, and grammar.

Compare the following two passages to see how the paraphrase differs from the original passage.

Original passage

> Recent research has determined that humans tend to fall into one of four quadrants according to their learning styles. Quadrant one learners tend to be divergent thinkers and need personal and emotional involvement in order for learning to take place. As idea people, they function through social integration and strive to bring unity to diversity. Quadrant two learners are assimilators, needing systematic learning via a logical and intellectual approach. As analytic learners, they reflect on ideas to create concepts and models. Quadrant three learners tend to be convergent thinkers who are practical, problem-oriented people. Pragmatic decision makers, they restrict judgment to concrete things. Quadrant four learners are accommodators needing random patterns of learning. They aim to bring action to concepts and exercise authority through common vision, hesitating to make decisions affecting others.

Paraphrase

> As learners, we fall into four groups. The first kind of learner needs to be caught up in an idea physically and personally. His personal involvement and concern for others make him seek harmony. He's emotional. The second kind of learner absorbs all the information around him, categorizes it, and reasons out the results. He will seek the data gathered to develop an idea. He's systematic. The third kind of learner is the opposite of the first. He tends to be less emotional, more utilitarian. His thorough analysis results in a valid decision. He's practical. The fourth kind of learner needs numerous approaches to learning something new. As an opposite to the second kind of learner, he relies more on instinct than on logic. When decisions must be made, he doesn't like to interfere with other's lives. He's an accommodator.

Notice the following details about the model paraphrase:

- The paraphrase presents the same ideas in the same order as the original passage and is nearly the same length.
- The vocabulary is quite different from that of the original. This change marks the most important function: to reduce technical or complicated writing to simpler, easier-to-understand prose.
- Complicated ideas are presented in short, simple sentences to make them easier

to understand. Notice that although the two passages are about the same length, the paraphrase has fifteen sentences while the original passage has only nine.

- The paraphrase shows careful reading and thorough understanding of the original. No plagiarism has crept in.

Precis

The precis (pronounced *pray-see*) is a summary shorter than the original passage and shorter than a paraphrase. Generally, it is a condensation of the main points of a piece of writing. A precis of one page may well summarize the points presented in twenty-five pages of carefully supported detail. Similarly, a precis of a hundred words may restate what an author explains in three pages. Finally, a precis of a single sentence may summarize a paragraph or two.

A precis usually

- omits details, illustrations, and subordinate ideas, presenting instead the major ideas
- reduces the original passage by at least two-thirds
- indicates careful reading of the original passage
- portrays the original author's concept accurately, without adding personal bias
- follows the guidelines of standard grammar, usage, and mechanics by using strong, effective sentence structure.

Compare the following two passages that illustrate how an effective precis springs from a lengthy text.

Original passage

Wood is a universal material, and no one has ever been able to make a satisfactory count of its many uses. The Forest Products Laboratory, a research institution of the United States Forest Service, at Madison, Wisconsin, once undertook to make an official count of wood uses. When last announced, the number was more than 5,000 and the argument had only started over how general or how specific a use had to be to get on the list.

Just one, well-known, wood-cellulose plastic, including its conversion products, claims 25,000 uses—among them such different items as dolls' eyes and advertising signs. The use of wood fiber as the basis for such products is increasing every day.

Another important use of wood is paper for printing our books, magazines, and newspapers. A high point in our culture came less than a century ago with the discovery that wood fiber could take the place of cotton or linen in paper manufacture. Today we use more than 73 million tons of paper and board each year. Of this amount each person's annual share of all kinds of paper and board is about 660 pounds. When paper was made chiefly of rags, each person's annual share was less than 10 pounds.

Container board accounts for about a fourth of our paper and board use. Newsprint accounts for an additional 17 percent of paper use. The rest is used in a myriad of forms—writing paper; sanitary cartons for prunes, cereals, butter, ice cream; paper cups, plates, disposable napkins, towels, and handkerchiefs; wrapping paper for groceries, meats, and dry goods.

Precis

The Forest Products Laboratory, a research institution of the U.S. Forest Service, suggests over 5,000 uses for wood, but admittedly no one knows how to set the limits of specificity for the list. For instance, some wood fiber products alone can boast over 25,000 uses, including dolls' eyes and billboards. In another example, wood supplies annually more than 73 million tons of paper and board, used for everything from containers to newsprint, amounting to over 40 percent of paper use.

Note the following about the precis above:

- It reduces the original by about two-thirds.
- While it includes several specific examples, it mostly confines itself to main ideas.
- Statistics and sources are considered key words and thus appear in the precis just as they did in the original.
- The writer has achieved some organizational patterns not evident in the original and used transitions to clarify relationships. Note particularly *for instance* and *in another example*, which alert the reader that these two phrases show how hard it is to quantify the uses of wood. Should the industry list *paper products* as a single use or list each product as a separate use? Thus the precis writer achieves what the author of the original passage did not: helps the reader reach a conclusion about the various facts and figures.

POSSIBLE PITFALL

As you take notes, practice good summarizing techniques. Be particularly careful to avoid using another writer's words as if they were your own. Remember to use quotation marks around key phrases borrowed from your sources.

Chapter Five

Using Primary Research

Up to now, we have been talking only about secondary research: the research that examines previously published findings. Now we need to consider another kind of research: primary research. Primary research is the research that the writer himself conducts.

STEP 8: **PREWRITING—** CONDUCTING PRIMARY RESEARCH

Not every topic lends itself to primary research. Some topics, however, will benefit significantly from firsthand information: interviews, experiments, personal data gathering, audience experience, statistical analysis, and surveys.

If, for instance, your subject deals with air pollutants emitted from power-generating plants, excerpts from an interview with an EPA official or with an official from a power plant will add perspective to your paper. Books, magazines, and periodicals are never as immediate as firsthand experience. Similarly, if your subject deals with the psychological problems of nursing-home residents, survey results will give credibility to your paper. Finally, if your subject deals with the best methods for storing fresh vegetables, a tabulation of the results of your own experiments will add an important dimension to your paper.

Use primary research whenever the subject suggests. For instance, Alicia had some experience with the care of Alzheimer's patients as a result of her volunteer work at a nursing home. When she began her research, she decided to interview the head of the Alzheimer's unit. You can see the results of that interview in her paper.

Consider how primary research can enhance your own paper.

Chapter Six

Drafting the Paper

Okay! Your research is finished; your note-taking, complete. You're ready to create the final plan, the first step in drafting your paper.

STEP 9: **WRITING—** CREATING THE FINAL PLAN

Begin with your note cards. Use the slugs to sort the cards into piles, each pile representing a topic on your revised outline. Next, sort through each pile, thinking about order.

Will *chronological order* be best? If there is some kind of time relationship involved in your subject, your paper probably needs to reflect it. For instance, if Alicia is showing the progression of Alzheimer's disease, chronological order is a natural.

Is *spatial order* better? If your subject involves some kind of relationship within a given space (top to bottom, left to right, front to back), you may need to use this organizational pattern for some segment of your paper. For instance, if you are analyzing a Civil War battle, you will need to help your reader visualize spatial relationships among the troops.

Will some *order of importance* make more sense? Sometimes the only way to arrange a series of details is according to their relative importance. If you are giving four reasons for something, put the *most important* reason last: It will remain with your reader longer. Use the second most important reason first: You begin with strength. Put other reasons in the middle, from more to less important. A *problem-solution* paper usually arranges its solutions in order of importance.

Will a *comparison-contrast* paper determine order? If you are comparing items, you have three choices for order:

* whole-by-whole
* part-by-part
* likenesses-differences

Which organization you use depends entirely on which works best for the subject. Assume a writer is discussing the methods of disciplining children. He plans to include three details: nonverbal messages, verbal messages, and reward/reinforcement. Compare the three orders:

Whole-by-whole

First method of discipline
  Nonverbal messages
  Verbal messages
  Reward/reinforcement

Second method of discipline
  Nonverbal messages
  Verbal messages
  Reward/reinforcement

Part-by-part

Nonverbal messages
  First method of discipline
  Second method of discipline
Verbal messages
  First method of discipline
  Second method of discipline

Reward/reinforcement
  First method of discipline
  Second method of discipline

Likenesses-differences, whole-by-whole

Similarities
  First method of discipline
    Nonverbal messages
    Verbal messages
    Reward/reinforcement
  Second method of discipline
    Nonverbal messages
    Verbal messages
    Reward/reinforcement

Differences
  First method of discipline
    Nonverbal messages
    Verbal messages
    Reward/reinforcement
  Second method of discipline
    Nonverbal messages
    Verbal messages
    Reward/reinforcement

Likenesses-differences, whole-by-whole

Similarities
  Nonverbal messages
    First method of discipline
    Second method of discipline
  Verbal messages
    First method of discipline
    Second method of discipline
  Reward/reinforcement
    First method of discipline
    Second method of discipline

Differences
  Nonverbal messages
    First method of discipline
    Second method of discipline
  Verbal messages
    First method of discipline
    Second method of discipline
  Reward/reinforcement
    First method of discipline
    Second method of discipline

Will a *combination* of orders be necessary? While every paper maintains an overall organizational plan, separate paragraphs may follow other orders. For instance, even if you are arranging your overall paper in order of importance, you may have certain supporting details in chronological order or cause/effect order. Use combinations as appropriate.

When you think your organizational plan makes sense, return to your outline. Expand or alter the outline as your note cards now suggest. If you have not already done so, add subtopics to your outline as suggested by the slugs.

For comparison's sake, look at Alicia's final outline. Compare it with her preliminary outline (page 23) and her later outline (page 28) to see how her note-taking guided the development of her outline.

When Alzheimer's Hits Home

Thesis sentence: Teenagers face a tough challenge in understanding and dealing with a loved one afflicted with Alzheimer's disease and who is regressing through cognitive deterioration, communication impairments, and behavior problems.

   I. Understanding the patient's cognitive deterioration
      A. Typical characteristics
         1. Coping with the regression
         2. Experiencing the effects
      B. Suitable responses
  II. Understanding the patient's communication impairments
      A. Typical characteristics
         1. Memory
         2. Comprehension
      B. Suitable responses
 III. Understanding the patient's behavioral problems
      A. Typical characteristics
         1. Verbal
         2. Physical
      B. Suitable responses
         1. Understanding
         2. Adaptation
 IV. Getting additional help
      A. To understand the patient
      B. To address personal fears

At this point, your final outline should nearly write itself. If your instructor requires a formal outline, use the following guidelines, most of which are illustrated in Alicia's outline above. An outline

- includes a title
- usually begins with a thesis statement
- includes topics or sentences, but not both
- follows a parallel structure
- uses a combination of Roman numerals, upper- and lowercase letters, and Arabic numbers to show relationships in the following pattern:
    Roman numerals
    capital letters
    Arabic numbers
    lowercase letters
    Arabic numbers followed by parentheses
    lowercase letters followed by parentheses
- shows the logic of development, so that the summary of the parts of any one subdivision equals the topic of that division
- will include topics that are mutually exclusive
- will include at least two divisions at any level, so that an item designated *1* will be followed by *2* and an item designated *a* will be followed by *b*
- guides the paragraph structure of a written paper, with each main idea or subheading representing a separate paragraph
- uses periods and parentheses to set number and letter designations apart from the outline topics or sentences
- follows a pattern of indentation to show the relationship of ideas, set up so that the Roman numerals have a ragged left margin and the periods after them align vertically
- capitalizes the first word of the sentence in a sentence outline or the first word of each topic in a topic outline
- includes a period at the end of each sentence in a sentence outline, but *not* after words or phrases in a topic outline

POSSIBLE PITFALLS

Whether or not you must submit a formal outline, keep these points in mind as you develop the outline that will guide your writing:

- A full-length research paper probably should have no more than four or five main points. This means you should have no more than four or five Roman numerals in your outline. Too many main headings indicate fuzzy thinking.
- The outline divisions correspond to paragraph divisions or to subtopics within the paragraphs. To determine whether the organization is logical, think through your outline in terms of paragraphs. (Compare Alicia's outline above with the paragraphs in her final paper beginning on page 75.)
- The outline divisions, added together, must equal your thesis sentence. If they do not, make whatever adjustments are necessary, either to the outline or to the thesis sentence.

STEP 10: **WRITING—** DEVELOPING THE FIRST DRAFT

With your revised outline and organized note cards in front of you, you are ready to write the first draft.

Technology Note

Keep a hard copy of every draft. Even though you may eventually toss them all, you will have something to turn to in the event of a hardware or software malfunction. In addition, writers often decide several drafts later to retrieve a discarded idea or paragraph. If you keep copies of each of your drafts, you will avoid possible disappointment and frustration.

The research paper, like a good theme, begins with an introductory paragraph. This introduces the subject and leads to the thesis sentence. In addition, however, it needs to attract the reader's attention and set the tone for the paper. Consider one of the following approaches for your introduction:

Say something startling, either by making a statement or by giving statistics.

Example:

> **To form one cubic inch of stalactite, that stone icicle found hanging from cave ceilings, nature requires about one hundred years.**

This statistic startles the reader who has seen stalactites the diameter of a human body dropping twenty or more feet from a cave ceiling. The writer can now proceed with her paper about the importance of protecting cave formations.

Describe a compelling scene or situation.

Example:

One week before St. Patrick's Day, the plane touched down at London's Heathrow International Airport. A train would take the tour group to Devonshire, the land of rolling hills and centuries-old stone fences. Settled into their coaches, the group relaxed and let busy London glide past them, as they slipped into something more comfortable—the rural pastoral English spring.

The scene helps the reader identify with the mood and perhaps arouses some curiosity. What happens to the tour group? The writer has introduced a paper about Romantic poets.

Refer to an event, either historical or current, perhaps in the form of a story or conversation.

Example:

A year ago this month, Jerrod Hunt graduated from high school. He and his friends celebrated even before the formal ceremony, but the real celebration came afterward. Today, Jerrod is trying desperately to learn to walk again.

The reader anticipates what has happened to Jerrod, and the writer has an effective attention-getting device to introduce his paper on alcoholism among teens.

Show a controversy, contradiction, or unusual opinion.

Example:

Despite computerized technology and presorted, zip-coded mail, most of us open first an envelope with a handwritten address.

The writer poses a contradiction between technology and the personal touch, thus catching the reader's attention for a paper on the need to revive the importance of personal letter writing.

Ask a question.

Example:

What keeps woodpeckers from destroying their brains when they pound relentlessly on wood?

A thought-provoking question serves as an attention-getter in this paper on ornithology.

Use a quotation, adage, or proverb.

Example:

Eric Hoffer wrote, "In times of change, learners inherit the earth, while the learned find themselves beautifully equipped to deal with a world that no longer exists."

The reader recognizes that the writer is about to address the need not for knowledge of facts but for knowledge of how to find out what one needs to know. The writer thus introduces his topic on the need for school curriculum reform.

With the introduction in place, use a transition to move into the body of your paper. The body follows the organization established in the outline, the divisions corresponding directly to the paragraphs. Use transitional devices within and between paragraphs to help the reader follow your thoughts. You may use

- **transitional words** *like thus, indeed, also, however, nevertheless, whereas, again, consequently, etc.*
- **transitional phrases** *like as a result, in turn, in addition to, because of this, in spite of, etc.*
- **transitional clauses** *like when the time came, after the course was over, since there was no evidence, because the circumstances warranted it, although the coach questioned him, etc.*
- **transitional sentences** (See the model paper.)
- **transitional paragraphs** (See the model paper.)

The final transition moves to the concluding paragraph. The conclusion should refer to the thesis sentence, wrap up the main ideas, and somehow return to the attention-getting device. The reader must feel that he/she has reached completion.

Beyond the typical content and organization of a good theme, the first draft of a research paper also includes one feature peculiar to the form:

MATERIAL FROM YOUR NOTE CARDS MUST BE ACKNOWLEDGED BY SOURCE, *WHETHER YOU PUT THE IDEA IN YOUR OWN WORDS OR QUOTE IT DIRECTLY.*

As a result, each time you refer to a note card in your first draft, add in parentheses the coded reference from the top righthand corner of your card (the bibliography source and page number). For example, study these two excerpts from Alicia's first draft:

Example: *Quoted material*

The disease referred to as the "dementing thief of minds and destroyer of personalities" (18-2) so dramatically changes a loved one that families struggle to cope.

The sentence includes a quoted passage that came from bibliography source 18 on page 2; thus the coded reference (18-2). Later, Alicia will convert the coded note into a formal documentation note.

Example: *Summarized material*

As a result, they may want to dress at odd hours, want to leave as soon as they arrive somewhere, think they have been left alone for days or weeks when it is only for a few minutes (6-16-17).

The idea is summarized in Alicia's own words, but the information came from bibliography source 6 on pages 16-17. The documentation is mandatory.

By using this simple coded note, you can move rapidly through the first draft without the burden of developing an exact form of documentation. During the revising process, you will finalize the formal documentation.

Complete the first draft as quickly as you can, working to get the ideas on paper. You need not necessarily write fine sentences or model paragraphs. Follow the outline, using the yo-yo approach, revising the outline, if necessary, altering the methods of organization, and adding essential supporting details.

STEP 11: **REVISING—** POLISHING THE CONTENT

When you have completed the first draft, polish its content.

- Make sure the introduction accomplishes what it should: Does it begin with an attention-getting device? Does it include a general statement about your subject? Does it bring readers from the general to the specific?

- Check the thesis statement for completeness and accuracy. Does it state or suggest the topics of each of the body paragraphs in your paper? Does it state or imply the order in which the ideas will appear?

- Be sure the paper follows the organization established in the thesis sentence.

- Check for good paragraph structure. Do you have a clear topic sentence for each paragraph? Have you included adequate developmental details for each paragraph?

Because many student researchers have to struggle to develop paragraphs adequately, you will want to compare the following two passages to understand what we mean by "adequate supporting details":

Original Passage

In spring, the fishermen replace the hunters on Hovey Lake waters. They come to catch big stringers of fish. Some are more successful than others. They use all kinds of methods to try to catch fish. Only when the lake closes do the fishermen leave.

Revised to Add Supporting Detail

In spring, the fishermen replace the hunters on Hovey Lake waters. Attracted by the spring crappie run, fishermen haul in hefty stringers of slabs and return to fish for bluegill. Evening campfires turn skillets full of fresh fillets into plates full of succulent morsels. Sunrise sends the bass fishermen slipping into secret waters, only a few returning with empty bags. Later, trotlines snare spoonbill catfish, those prehistoric monsters weighing thirty pounds or more, some as long as a man is tall. In late afternoon or early evening, jug fishermen bag perch, catfish, or even a wily gar, long, slender, and sharp-toothed. So the routine goes. Spring moves into summer, and summer moves into autumn. Only then, when the lake closes for waterfowl migration, do the fishermen leave.

- Make certain you have included a sufficient number of transitions within and between paragraphs. Compare the following two passages to see what is meant by "sufficient transitions":

Original Passage

Candidates see the depressed economy as a major issue in the eighth district. Brolliette proposes tax incentives to lure big businesses into the area. The incumbent voted for the huge tax incentive that brought two moderate-sized businesses to the area. Citizens have been hit with major increases in their personal property tax bills. The businesses created over 1,200 jobs. Almost all the jobs have gone to employees who accepted a transfer. One business' plant closed in the Southwest. Irate citizens are footing the tax bill for jobs not open to them. Brolliette defends the position. Kinsingtonne warned city and county councils two years ago that citizens would face the increase. He fought for citizen protection before he announced his candidacy for office. He understands the working man's plight and the ramifications of big business on the little man's pocketbook.

Revised to Include Transitions

Each candidate sees the depressed economy as a major issue in the eighth district. *On the one hand,* Brolliette proposes tax incentives to lure big businesses in the area. *In fact,* the incumbent voted for the huge tax incentive that brought two moderate-sized businesses to the area. *Suddenly, as a result,* area citizens have been hit with major increases in their personal property tax bills, some as much as double. *Although* the businesses have created over 1,200 jobs, almost all have gone to employees who accepted a transfer as a result of one business' plant closing in the Southwest. *Thus,* irate citizens are footing a tax bill for jobs *seemingly* not open to them. Brolliette *nevertheless continues* to defend the position. Kinsingtonne, *on the other hand,* warned city and county councils two years ago that citizens would face the increase. He fought for citizen protection even before he announced his candidacy for office. *Apparently* he understands the working man's plight. And *apparently he understands better than Brolliette* the ramifications of big business on the little man's pocketbook.

• Be sure you have maintained unity by omitting any unrelated material. Some student writers feel driven to include every bit of information entered on a note card. In order to maintain unity, you may need to discard certain notes. Ask yourself these questions: In every paragraph, does every sentence tell something about the topic sentence? Does every paragraph in some way explain the thesis sentence?

Compare the two following passages that demonstrate how to revise a paragraph to give it unity:

Original passage

Nearly every community tries to combat the problems pigeons create. While pigeons are docile and provide enjoyment in the parks for those who like to feed them peanuts and popcorn, they also create a health hazard where they most frequently roost. Some experts try simply to change the roosting place. Of course, that only causes the health hazard to relocate. In fact, one year, officials used chicken wire to close off a favorite roosting place; so the pigeons began roosting in our garage. They created not only a health hazard but a financial burden as well. We had to have the car repainted as a result of the frequent stains on the hood. In spite of that, I really like pigeons. In fact, we used to raise pigeons when I was a child. Some of them are quite beautiful, not only because of their colors but also because of the ruffs around their necks or the long feathers along their legs. Of course, these are special breeds.

Revised to maintain unity

Nearly every community tries to combat the problems pigeons create. While docile pigeons provide enjoyment for those who like to feed them peanuts and popcorn in the parks, they also create a health hazard where they most frequently roost. In addition, they deface buildings, monuments, and other public and private properties. To alleviate the problems, some communities erect wire barriers around the pigeons' favorite roosting places. Nearly invisible, the wire tends to be the least offensive relief measure. Other communities try various noise-makers to scare the birds from the roosts. Sirens, clappers, gunshots, and mild explosions send the pigeons on their way. Of course, the noise disturbs human residents as well, so to some the solution seems more unpleasant than the problem. With either means of combating the problem, however, the pigeons simply move elsewhere. As a result, the problem does not go away; it merely relocates.

• Reread for good sentence structure and sentence variety.

Compare the following two passages that illustrate how to create good sentence structure and sentence variety:

Original Passage

Biologists have been studying the balance of nature at Isle Royale National Park. It is an unusual experiment. The park contains 210 square miles of wilderness. Scientists can study animal relationships there. The animals are not disturbed by man or other animals. Moose arrived on the island early this century. They probably came by swimming from the Canadian shore. The moose multiplied because they had no predators. They literally ate themselves out of house and home. They could not leave the island. They starved. They died in large numbers. A fire in 1936 nearly eliminated the browsing food moose eat. It was a disaster. The fire, in turn, opened large areas for new growth. The new growth was just the right diet for the huge animals. The herd grew. It outgrew its supply of food again.

Revised to Include Sentence Variety

For the past fifty years biologists have been studying the balance of nature by means of a unique experiment conducted in the self-contained laboratory called Isle Royale National Park. The park, an island consisting of 210 square miles of wilderness, affords scientists the opportunity to observe animal relationships in an environment completely undisturbed by man. Sometime early in this century, moose arrived on the island, probably by swimming from the Canadian shore. By the early 1930s, proliferating without predators, the moose herds literally ate themselves out of house and home. Limited by the boundaries of the island, they starved, dying in large numbers. A disastrous fire in 1936 nearly eliminated the browsing food moose eat; but in turn, the fire opened large areas for new growth, just the right diet for the huge animals. So the herd grew. Again it outgrew its supply of food.

Note the following details about the revised passage:

The sentences vary from four words to thirty words. Since the longest and shortest sentences appear next to one another, the juxtaposition puts emphasis on the idea in the short sentence.

The sentences vary in structure from simple sentences to compound-complex sentences.

The sentences include a wide variety of modifiers: single words, phrases, and clauses.

The sentences begin in a variety of ways: with prepositional phrases, participial phrases, subjects, transitional words and phrases, relative pronouns, and introductory clauses.

Technology Note

Certain software programs offer what are generically called "style check-ers." These programs, while not foolproof, will analyze sentence length, highlight subordinating conjunctions, check for frequency of transitions, etc. You may find this analysis helpful.

- Assure yourself that your subject is fully and carefully explained and that it is supported with adequate research.
- Be sure the conclusion reiterates the thesis sentence and adds an appropriate clincher. Using a clincher that refers to the introductory attention-getter gives the reader the best sense of completeness, a feeling of having seen the full picture.
- Finally, add a title. Try to create one that attracts attention and captures the reader's imagination.

When you have made these improvements to the content of your paper, you are ready to tackle the details of preparing the final draft.

Chapter Seven

Preparing the Documentation

The forms of documentation required for your research paper will vary with the style manual preferred by the instructor. The most important principle, however, is to use a consistent documentation style throughout the paper.

In Chapter Nine, you will find illustrated five common research paper styles. The complete sample paper illustrates the most commonly used style; parts of the same paper are repeated to illustrate four other styles:

1. **MLA (Modern Language Association) parenthetical style:** documentation notes appear parenthetically within the text.

2. **MLA endnote style:** documentation notes appear at the end of the paper, just before the list of works cited.

3. **MLA footnote style:** documentation notes appear at the bottoms of the pages.

4. **MLA numbered bibliography style:** documentation notes appear in numerical form, parenthetically, within the text.

5. **APA (American Psychological Association) style:** documentation notes appear parenthetically, within the text.

Use whichever form of notation your instructor requires; or, if no specific form is required, use the one easiest for you. In any case, be consistent throughout the paper.

STEP 12: **REVISING—** PREPARING FINAL DOCUMENTATION NOTES

Whether you use parenthetical notes, endnotes, or footnotes, you will follow a prescribed form. Each is detailed here.

Parenthetical Notes

Parenthetical notes follow this simple format:

- Enclose parenthetical notes in parentheses.
- Place notes immediately after quoted material or at the end of paraphrased material.
- Include in a parenthetical note only the author's or editor's last name(s) and the page reference.
- Omit any punctuation between the name(s) and the page reference.
- If you cite more than one work by an author, list the author's name followed by a comma, the title (shortened version if practical), and page numbers.

Examples:

> (Johnson 176)
> (Collins and Robards 28)

- If the note refers to material for which no author is credited, use the title, or a shortened version of the title, in quotation marks (for articles and pamphlets) or underlined (for books), and the page reference.

Example:

> ("Saving" 14)

This abbreviated form of the title refers readers to an article titled "Saving the Whales: What Can Legislators Do?"

Endnotes or Footnotes

If, instead of parenthetical documentation, you use endnotes or footnotes, follow the same form for either. Note these peculiarities:

- Number endnotes and footnotes consecutively throughout the paper.
- Raise the numbers, writing them as superscript, both in the text and in the notes themselves.

- Indent the notes like paragraphs.
- Follow notes with periods as if they were complete sentences.
- Type footnotes single-spaced with double space between notes.
- Type endnotes double-spaced.

Sample note forms are listed on pages 90 and 94, along with their corresponding bibliography formats.

STEP 13: **REVISING—**
PREPARING THE FINAL BIBLIOGRAPHY

A bibliography is always part of a research paper. It may also be called a list of works cited or a list of references. No matter its label, it will be one of two kinds: a list of only those works actually cited in the paper; or a list of all works consulted, some of which may not have been cited.

The advantage of the former is its brevity; the advantage of the latter is its demonstration of thorough research. Use whichever form your instructor prefers.

Whichever bibliography you prepare, follow these general guidelines:

- Begin the bibliography on a new page at the end of the paper.
- Arrange the entries alphabetically by authors' last names.
- If a work is unsigned, alphabetize by the title. If the first word is one of the articles, *a*, *an*, or *the*, alphabetize by the second word. Move the article, preceded by a comma, to the end of the title.

Example:

"License to Hunt: Photographers' Privileges, A."

- Use hanging indentation for the bibliography; that is, indent all lines but the first. This format allows for ease in finding individual entries.
- Follow each item in the bibliography with a period, as if each were a separate sentence.
- Give each note a corresponding bibliography entry.
- Type the bibliography double-spaced. A less-common style uses single spacing with double spacing between entries.
- If you cite two works by the same author, alphabetize by the title of the work. Do not list the author's name in front of the second work; instead, use three hyphens followed by a period.

Examples:

Kelley, Johnathan. <u>Recognizing Winning Work Habits</u>. New York: Jason Publishing Co.,
 1995.

—<u>Winning Sales in Tough Competition</u>. Chicago: Minney, Coleson, Inc., 1994.

Additional details of format are noted in the examples below.

NOTE AND BIBLIOGRAPHY FORMS

For Books

In general, a note or bibliography entry for a book includes the author's name, the
book title italicized (underlined), and the publication information (city of publication, publisher, and date). The note, but not the bibliography entry, will include a
page reference. In a bibliography list, books are arranged alphabetically by their
respective authors' or editors' last names. The samples below include bibliography
forms, parenthetical-note forms, and endnote forms. (See additional examples in
the model papers in Chapter Nine.) Footnotes appear in the same form as endnotes
but are single-spaced, with a double space between entries.

Book by one author

Bibliography:
Lannon, John M. <u>Technical Writing</u>. Boston: Little, Brown and Company, 1982.

Parenthetical note:
(Lannon 139)

Endnote:
 [1] John M. Lannon, <u>Technical Writing</u> (Boston: Little, Brown and Company, 1982)
139.

Book by two authors

Bibliography:
Gibaldi, Joseph, and Walter S. Achtert. <u>MLA Handbook for Writers of Research Papers</u>.
 3rd ed. New York: The Modern Language Association of America, 1988.

Parenthetical note:
(Gibaldi and Achtert 140)

Endnote:
    ² Joseph Gibaldi and Walter S.Achtert, <u>MLA Handbook for Writers of Research Papers</u>, 3rd ed. (New York: The Modern Language Association of America, 1988) 140.

Note: The above entries refer to the *third edition* of a book. The publisher is an organization.

Book by three or more authors

Bibliography:
Frew, Robert, and others. <u>Survival: A Sequential Program for College Writing</u>. Palo Alto, Calif.: Peek Publications, 1978.

Parenthetical note:
(Frew and others 111-112)

Endnote:
    ³ Robert Frew and others, <u>Survival: A Sequential Program for College Writing</u> (Palo Alto, Calif.: Peek Publications, 1978) 111-112.

Notes:

1. If the name of the city is not widely recognized, the state should be listed as well, using the standard abbreviation not the two-letter postal form.

2. Some style manuals allow the abbreviation "et al." instead of "and others." Either is correct, although "and others" is more readily recognized by readers.

3. Compare this set of entries for two or more authors with those for a book with two or more editors. When three authors or editors are named, different style manuals allow either form, i.e., you may use all three names or just the words "and others." All style manuals, however, use "and others" for four or more authors or editors.

Book with an editor

Bibliography:
Williams, Becky Hall, ed. <u>1995 Writer's Market: Where to Sell What You Write</u>. Cincinnati: Writer's Digest Books, 1995.

Parenthetical note:
(Williams 925)

Endnote:
        [4] Becky Hall Williams, ed., <u>1995 Writer's Market: Where to Sell What You</u>
<u>Write</u> (Cincinnati: Writer's Digest Books, 1995) 925.

Book with two or more editors

Bibliography:
Polking, Kirk, Joan Bloss, and Colleen Cannon, eds. <u>Writer's Encyclopedia</u>. Cincinnati:
        Writer's Digest Books, 1983.

Parenthetical note:
(Polking and others 178)

Endnote:
        [5] Kirk Polking, Joan Bloss, and Colleen Cannon, eds., <u>Writer's Encyclopedia</u>
(Cincinnati: Writer's Digest Books, 1983) 178.

Book by a corporate author

Bibliography:
The Reader's Digest Association, Inc. <u>America the Beautiful</u>. Pleasantville, N.Y.: The
        Reader's Digest Association, Inc., 1970.

Parenthetical note:
(Reader's Digest Assoc. 47-48)

Endnote:
        [6] The Reader's Digest Association, Inc., <u>America the Beautiful</u> (Pleasantville,
N.Y.: The Reader's Digest Association, Inc., 1970) 47-48.

Multivolume work

Bibliography:
Highland, Harold Joseph. <u>Encyclopedia of Space Science</u>. Illustrated ed. 2 vols. New
        York: Theodore Audel and Company, 1963.

Parenthetical note:
(Highland 711)

Endnote:
⁷ Harold Joseph Highland, <u>Encyclopedia of Space Science</u>, Illustrated ed. vol. I (New York: Theodore Audel and Company, 1963) 711.

Signed encyclopedia article

Bibliography:
von Brandt, Andres R. F. T. "Fishing, Commercial." <u>Encyclopaedia Britannica: Macropaedia</u>. 1983 ed.

Parenthetical note:
(von Brandt)

Endnote:
⁸ Andres R. F. T. von Brandt, "Fishing, Commercial," <u>Encyclopaedia Britannica: Macropaedia</u>, 1983 ed.

Unsigned article in reference book

Bibliography:
"Crowley, Robert." <u>Encyclopedia Americana</u>. 1984 ed.

Parenthetical note:
("Crowley")

Endnote:
⁹ "Crowley, Robert," <u>Encyclopedia Americana</u>, 1984 ed.

Selection in an anthology

Bibliography:
Winters, Yvor. "Robert Frost: Or the Spiritual Drifter as Poet." <u>Robert Frost: A Collection of Critical Essays</u>. Ed. James M. Cox. Englewood Cliffs, N.J.: Prentice-Hall, Inc., 1962.

Parenthetical note:
(Winters 59-60)

Endnote:
¹⁰ Yvor Winters, "Robert Frost: Or the Spiritual Drifter as Poet," in <u>Robert Frost: A Collection of Critical Essays</u>, ed. James M. Cox (Englewood Cliffs, N.J.: Prentice-Hall, Inc., 1962) 59-60.

Translation

Bibliography:
Vergilius Maro, Publius. <u>Virgil</u>. Trans. H. Rushton Fairclough. Rev. ed. Cambridge: Harvard
   University Press, 1935.

Parenthetical note:
(Vergilius 48)

Endnote:
       [11] Publius Vergilius Maro, <u>Virgil</u>, trans. H. Rushton Fairclough, rev. ed. (Cambridge: Harvard University Press, 1935) 48.

For Periodicals

In general, the information included in both bibliography and note forms for periodicals will be the author's name, the name of the article in quotation marks, the name of the periodical italicized (underlined), the date of publication, and the page reference. In a bibliography list, periodicals are arranged alphabetically by the author's last name. If the periodical includes no author's name, then the work is alphabetized by the first word of the article's title, ignoring the articles *a, an,* and *the*. The samples below include a bibliography form and parenthetical and endnote forms. (See additional examples in the model papers in Chapter Nine.)

Signed article in a monthly periodical

Bibliography:
Rupp, Becky. "Home Schooling." <u>Country Journal</u> December 1986: 67-74.

Parenthetical note:
(Rupp 67)

Endnote:
       [12] Becky Rupp, "Home Schooling." <u>Country Journal</u> December 1986: 67.

Article in a bimonthly periodical

Bibliography:
Schwartz, David M. "Hurray for Hedgehogs!" <u>International Wildlife</u> Mar.-Apr. 1990:
   22-27.

Parenthetical note:
(Schwartz 24)

Endnote:
    [13] David M. Schwartz, "Hurray for Hedgehogs!" <u>International Wildlife</u> Mar.-Apr. 1990: 24.

Article in a weekly or biweekly periodical

Bibliography:
Gentry, Calloway, and K. Eisterholt. "The Great Cats." <u>Business Week</u> 4 June 1990: 101-104.

Parenthetical note:
(Gentry and Eisterholt 101)

Endnote:
    [14] Calloway Gentry and K. Eisterholt, "The Great Cats." <u>Business Week</u> 4 June 1990: 101.

Unsigned periodical article

Bibliography:
"The S.A.D. Truth about Sunlight." <u>Harrowsmith</u> November/December 1986: 123.

Parenthetical note:
("S.A.D. Truth" 123)

Endnote:
    [15] "The S.A.D. Truth about Sunlight." <u>Harrowsmith</u> November/December 1986: 123.

Article from a daily newspaper

Bibliography:
Reibstein, Larry. "A Finger on the Pulse: Companies Expand Use of Employee Surveys." <u>The Wall Street Journal</u> 27 October 1986, midwest ed.: 23.

Parenthetical note:
(Reibstein 23)

Endnote:
      [16] Larry Reibstein, "A Finger on the Pulse: Companies Expand Use of Employee Surveys." The Wall Street Journal 27 October 1986, midwest ed.: 23.

Note: The arrangement of the date is peculiar to the form: the day appears before the month and year.

Unsigned newspaper article

Bibliography:
"Save Vanishing Rain Forests." The Hoosier Quarterly News Fall 1995: 3.

Parenthetical note:
("Save Forests" 3)

Endnote:
      [17] Save Vanishing Rain Forests." The Hoosier Quarterly News Fall 1995: 3.

Letter to the editor

Bibliography:
Henley, Laura. Letter. The Newburgh Gazette 19 May 1995: 7.

Parenthetical note:
(Henley 7)

Endnote:
      [18] Laura Henley, letter, The Newburgh Gazette 9 May 1995: 7.

Pamphlet

Bibliography:
Geologic Story of Turkey Run State Park. Bloomington, Indiana: State of Indiana Department of Natural Resources Geological Survey, 1977.

Parenthetical note:
(Geologic Story 2)

Endnote:
      [19] Geologic Story of Turkey Run State Park (Bloomington, Indiana: State of Indiana Department of Natural Resources Geological Survey, 1977) 2.

Radio or television program

Bibliography:
<u>Nightly News</u>. Writ. Lloyd Winnecke. PBS. WKOP, Bloomdale 11 Sept. 1995.

Parenthetical note:
(<u>Nightly News</u>)

Endnote:
     [20] <u>Nightly News</u>, writ. Lloyd Winnecke, PBS, WKOP, Bloomdale 11 Sept. 1995.

Letter

Bibliography:
Romick, Lucinda. Letter to the author. 12 Dec. 1994.

Parenthetical note:
(Romick)

Endnote:
     [21] Lucinda Romick, letter to the author, 12 Dec. 1994.

Interview

Bibliography:
Casey, Charles. Personal interview. 11 Nov. 1995.

Parenthetical note:
(Casey)

Endnote:
     [22] Charles Casey, personal interview, 11 Nov. 1995.

Map or chart

Bibliography:
<u>Kansas</u>. Map. Chicago: Rand McNally, 1983.

Parenthetical note:
(Kansas)

Endnote:
    [23] <u>Kansas</u>, map (Chicago: Rand McNally, 1983).

Lecture, speech, or address

Bibliography:
Harris, Muriel. Address. Opening General Sess. NMSC Annual Convention. Kansas
    City, Kan., 14 May 1990.

Parenthetical note:
(Harris)

Endnote:
    [24] Muriel Harris, address, Opening General Sess., NMSC Annual Convention,
Kansas City, Kan., 14 May 1990.

Survey or experiment

Bibliography:
Ruminer, Carlton. "Survey of Nursing Home Residents' Attitudes Toward Activities." St.
    Joseph, Ill., 21-26 Oct. 1995.

Parenthetical note:
(Ruminer)

Endnote:
    [25] Carlton Ruminer, "Survey of Nursing Home Residents' Attitudes Toward Ac-
tivities." St. Joseph, Ill., 21-26 Oct. 1995.

Government publication

Bibliography:
United States Department of Commerce. Bureau of the Census. <u>Neighborhood Statistics
    from the 1980 Census</u>. N.p.: N.p., n.d.

Parenthetical note:
(U.S. Dept. of Commerce 8-9)

Endnote:
    [26] United States Department of Commerce, Bureau of the Census, <u>Neighbor-
hood Statistics from the 1980 Census</u> (N.p.: N.p., n.d.) 8-9.

Note: The abbreviations *n.p.* and *n.d.* stand for "no publisher" or "no place of publication" and "no date." Use these abbreviations when the publication data is not included anywhere in the publication, a fairly common occurrence in pamphlets and brochures. Sometimes "no pagination" [n.p.] is necessary when pages have no numbers.

For a Second Endnote or Footnote from the Same Source

In the course of writing a paper, you will probably cite some sources more than once. The primary note forms illustrated above are simplified considerably for secondary notes: Generally, you will use only the author's last name and the page number.

First note
    [27] David Powell, <u>What Can I Write About? 7000 Topics for High School Students</u> (Urbana, Ill.: National Council of Teachers of English, 1981) 26.

Subsequent note
    [28] Powell 38.

If you use more than one work by an author, the subsequent note must also identify the work, but perhaps in a shortened form. Compare the following examples:

First note
    [29] David Powell, <u>What Can I Write About? 7000 Topics for High School Students</u> (Urbana, Ill.: National Council of Teachers of English, 1981) 26.

Second work by same author:
    [30] David Powell, <u>More Topics for High School Students</u> (Urbana, Ill.: National Council of Teachers of English, 1989) 12.

Subsequent notes
    [31] Powell, <u>What Can I Write About?</u>, 42.

    [32] Powell, <u>More Topics</u>, 48.

If the subsequent note refers to an unsigned work, use a shortened form of the title.

First note
    [33] "Working at Home via Your Modem." <u>Business Week</u> 18 June 1994: 17.

Subsequent note
    [34] "Working at Home." 19.

Note: The abbreviations *ibid.* and *op cit.,* terms formerly used in subsequent notes, are no longer common.

Chapter Eight

Preparing the Final Copy

Be sure to allow adequate time to prepare the final draft. All your work to date will be meaningless if your final copy is poorly done. (See the appropriate time management guidelines on pages 5-7.)

STEP 14: **REVISING—** FORMATTING THE FINAL DRAFT

The final draft, which should be printed with a letter-quality printer, demands careful attention to format details.

Use these guidelines for typing your paper:

General Formatting

- The entire paper, including quotations, notes, and bibliography, is double-spaced.
- Except for page numbers, use one-inch margins on all four sides of each page.
- Use a running head to number all pages consecutively, including the first page and the bibliography page(s). To create a running head, type your last name and the page number a half inch from the top of each page and flush with the right margin.

Technology Note

Your software probably includes a command that will automatically place a header at the right margin and include consecutive page numbering.

- All text begins a double space below the running head.

Format for First Page

- On the first page of text, create a heading as follows:
  At the left margin, type your name one inch from the top.
  On three subsequent double-spaced lines, type your instructor's name, the course title, and the date, using day-month-year order.
- Center the title a double space below the last line of the heading.
- Capitalize only the first letter of appropriate words in the title.
- Do not use quotation marks or underscores with the title.
- Begin the text a double space below the title.
- Indent five spaces for each new paragraph.
- See page 75 for a model.

Format for Parenthetical Documentation

- Insert parenthetical notes as necessary to credit sources of facts, ideas, statistics, and exact words. Remember that parenthetical notes refer readers to the bibliography and that they include only the author's last name and page number(s).
- Use no punctuation between the name and page number.
- If the author's name appears in the text, the parenthetical note includes only a page number.
- See Chapter Seven for details and the complete model in Chapter Nine for illustrations.

Format for Long Quotations

- If you use a quotation that requires more than four typed lines, set off the entire passage by indenting it ten spaces from the left margin.
- Type a long quotation double-spaced, without quotation marks. (Another, less popular, style for designating a long quotation is to indent it ten spaces from both left and right margins and type it single-spaced, without quotation marks. Use whichever style your instructor prefers.)
- See pages 75, 76, 79, 80-81, 83 for illustrations.

Format for Bibliography Page

- The bibliography page should have the title *Works Cited* (most common), *References*, or *Bibliography* (least common), centered.
- Double-space and begin the entries.

- Use hanging indentation.
- Double-space all entries.
- See pages 84-85 for a complete illustration.

Format for Endnotes

- Type the title, *Notes*, centered, one inch from the top of a new page.
- Begin the notes a double space below the title.
- Indent each note five spaces, type the note number slightly above the line (or use the "superscript" command, skip a space, and begin the note.
- Any additional lines for a note appear at the left margin.
- Double-space all.
- See page 90 for an illustration.

Format for Footnotes

- Begin two double spaces below the text.
- Arrange as for endnotes (see above), but single-space footnotes with a double space between.
- On the last page, if the text does not fill the page, space footnotes near the bottom.
- See page 94 for an illustration.

Format for Title Page

- If your instructor requires a title page, DO NOT use a title page along with the heading described above in "Format for First Page." *Instead* use the following format:
- On a separate page, center from top to bottom and left to right the following five items: title of the paper, your name, the name of the course, the instructor's name, and the date the paper is due.
- Do not number the title page.
- Repeat the title, centered, on the first page of the text.
- Skip four spaces and begin the text.
- Do not number the first page of the text.
- See page 92 for an illustration and compare the first page of this model with the first pages of other models.

Format for Outlines

- If your instructor requires an outline, type your final outline in standard indented form, on a separate page.
- Include the thesis statement at the head of your outline.
- If your instructor prefers, this outline may be rearranged to appear as a table of contents.
- Number the outline page(s) with lowercase Roman numerals, centered at the bottom of the page.
- See page 93 for an illustration.

These formatting details and the examples in Chapter Nine should help you prepare an attractive, clean paper. Just be sure to save time for the following step, the last in preparing a superior research paper.

STEP 15: **PROOFREADING—** CHECKING THE DETAILS

In addition to the usual checks for spelling, mechanics, grammar, and usage, you will want to check documentation forms carefully, period for period and comma for comma. Check for underscoring and quotation marks. Read carefully for typing errors.

Technology Note

If you use a spell checker and/or style checker, remember that neither is foolproof. For instance, a spell checker will not find wrong words, only misspelled words. You must read your paper carefully, even with the technological assistance.

The most important proofreading you will do for a research paper, however, is quite different from that for any other paper. As well as the aforementioned checks, you must pay particular attention to the accuracy of documentation: check quoted material, paraphrased material, and credits to the sources of both.

BE SURE TO CHECK THE USE OF QUOTATION MARKS FOR ANY
QUOTED MATERIAL YOU MAY HAVE INCLUDED IN YOUR PAPER.

Remember, if you use another author's words as if they were your own—even
accidentally—you can suffer severe penalties. Plagiarism is a serious error. You
should check your original sources against the ideas you have included in your
paper just to be certain you have not simply forgotten a set of quotation marks or
neglected to copy the quotation marks from your note cards into your paper.

Chapter Nine

Studying the Models

Five research paper samples follow. The first sample, which is a complete paper, illustrates the most widely accepted form for liberal arts studies, the MLA (Modern Language Association, 1988) parenthetical style. Rapidly becoming singularly popular, parenthetical documentation omits all superscript numbers, thus permitting the use of less-sophisticated word-processing software and printers.

The second sample, an excerpt from the first, illustrates the MLA endnote style, a common alternative to the MLA parenthetical style.

The third sample, also an excerpt from the first, shows the MLA footnote style. The sample also illustrates a title page, an outline page, footnote documentation, and a single-spaced bibliography page.

The fourth sample, another excerpt, illustrates the APA (American Psychological Association) style. Parenthetical documentation and mode of bibliography entries distinguish this style.

The fifth sample illustrates, in a brief paragraph, the MLA numbered bibliography style.

Certain style manuals will suggest a combination of these basic formats. For instance, you may be asked to include a title page and a table of contents in a paper documented with endnotes. Thus, combined, the five models illustrate the principles we have discussed and offer sound guidelines no matter the format you may be asked to follow.

If your instructor permits you to choose your own style, choose the easiest one to prepare.

Once you finish studying the model research papers, read the analysis that follows the one complete model. Apply these criteria to your own paper as you proofread one more time. Then you can submit your paper knowing that it is well done.

Alicia Perkins
Ms. R. O. Cooper
Senior English
14 January 20—

When Alzheimer's Hits Home

As a reflection of the human condition, early literature includes references to "old timer's" disease. Perhaps Shakespeare's King Lear best describes the malady when he says to his daughter Cordelia and her husband:

I fear I am not in my perfect mind.
Methinks I should know you, and know this man;
Yet I am doubtful; for I am mainly ignorant
What place this is; and all the skill I have
Remembers not these garments; nor I know not
Where I did lodge last night. Do not laugh at me.
(4.7. 63-68)

Lear no doubt suffers from the irreversible brain deterioration known today as Alzheimer's disease, or AD. Unnamed until 1906 when Alois Alzheimer described the condition ("Chronology" 625), AD, an organic disease that destroys brain cells, now affects up to four million Americans (<u>You Are Not Alone</u>). Within fifty years, predictions say that fourteen million sufferers will face the fourth leading cause of death in America (ADRDA, <u>Statistics</u> I).

When a relative has AD, however, statistics, frightening or not, take a back seat.The disease referred to as the "dementing thief of minds and destroyer of personalities" (Leroux 2) so dramatically changes a loved one that families struggle to cope; and among family members, young people face unique problems. In the midst of striving to understand their own changing adolescent roles, they may also find themselves striving to understand a changing grandparent. They face a tough challenge both to understand and to deal with the grandparent's cognitive deterioration, communication impairments, and behavior modifications.

Any form of dementia, AD being the worst, involves the "loss or impairment of mental powers" (Mace 5).The impairment begins slowly, almost imperceptibly: forgetting names, words, and later, meals; being unable to make change, balance a checkbook, or learn anything new; getting lost; forgetting the day or month. As the disease progresses, victims lose the ability to track time, even confusing day and night. As a result, they may want to dress at odd hours, want to leave as soon as they arrive somewhere, think they have been left alone for days or weeks when it is only for a few minutes ("Stages of AD" 16-17). "For the person with a memory impairment, life may be like constantly coming into the middle of a movie: one has no idea what happened just before what is happening now" (Mace 24). Perhaps Mary's case helps explain the loss of cognitive powers:

> Mary gradually lost the ability to make sense out of what her eyes and ears told her. Noises and confusion made her feel panicky. She couldn't understand, they couldn't explain, and often panic overwhelmed her. She worried about her things: a chair, and the china that had belonged to her mother. They said they had told her over and over, but she could not remember where her things had gone. Perhaps someone had stolen them. She had lost so much. What things she still had, she hid, but then she forgot where she hid them (Mace 3).

When a grandparent or other relative shows cognitive deficits, families face the frustration that in spite of the fact that Grandmother does not look sick, she is. She may lose the ability to dial the telephone, use a can opener, put on a sweater, tie her shoes, or distinguish between detergent and mouthwash. In this condition, "even the most minute change [in routine or environment] may lead to additional confusion and disorientation in the patient" (Powell

Perkins 3

145), changes like additional noise, additional people, or strangers. When Grandmother suffers such cognitive deficits, young people generally encounter more frustration than do other family members, for teens often like loud music, boisterous groups of peers, and crowds of friends over for an evening or weekend. If Grandmother lives with the family, her reaction may be rage, restlessness, confusion, or agitation. So, how does a teen cope with Grandmother's condition?

Research suggests that many times young people "have clever ideas about how to solve problems that the rest of the family may not have thought of" (Mace 187). Because of their youth and resilience, once teens come to grips with the reality of Grandmother's condition, they often know how to help. They seem to know intuitively, for instance, how to modify a task, to simplify rather than change it. The simplification lets Grandmother continue a relatively normal life. At the same time, teens can laugh when they find the curtain rod in the freezer (Powell 135). Their youth often renders them more sympathetic than older members of the family, and they readily recognize that "the patient must be treated with kindness and dignity while at the same time being watched like a young child . . . [needing] overt signs of love and warmth" (Tanner and Shaw 97-98).

Teens can be supportive, too, by spending time with Grandmother, taking her for a walk or for a visit with an old friend; helping her keep up social activities as much as possible; helping her feel needed; reading to her or getting talking books or records for her; taking her to the zoo, museum, park, or shopping center; and naming visitors and relatives to help her recognize and remember them (Cohen 148). Teens can substitute for Grandmother's cognitive deficits by verbalizing their own sensory perceptions: pointing out the sunset, birds singing, pretty flowers. Patients still enjoy such sensory experiences, but they may not be able to locate or isolate them without help (Mace 62). The best advice for teens dealing with Grandmother's cognitive deficits probably comes packaged in one sentence: AD is an unpredictable illness, so one must adjust as the patient develops new symptoms (Martinson, Chesla, and Muwaswes 230).

As AD progresses, Grandfather may face another frustrating symptom as his ability to communicate deteriorates. Not only does the patient lose his memory of the names of people and things, but he also loses the ability to make sense of others' words. Since reading and understanding involve two different brain functions, Grandfather may be able to read the note on the refrigerator that says his lunch is in the red bowl, but he does not eat lunch because he no longer understands the meaning of the words (Mace 31). So how can young people deal with Grandfather's steadily declining ability to understand and to be understood?

While very young children rarely talk about abstract topics and therefore can easily communicate with AD patients, unfortunately teens, more like adults, frequently become angry or frustrated when Grandfather can no longer speak coherently (Heston 137). Teens can best respond to communication problems with Grandfather by speaking quietly and calmly; maintaining eye contact; using short, simple, familiar words and sentences; asking only one question or giving only one direction at a time; using the same words and phrasing for repeated instructions; noticing Grandfather's emotions through his voice and gestures; pointing and encouraging him to point; and offering a guess when he cannot come up with a word (ADRDA, Communicating 3-5). When Grandfather becomes so severely confused that he can no longer communicate, nonverbal communication, or body language, conveys more to the AD victim than do words. One AD nurse suggests that teens try to enter the patient's world and become an empathetic listener, trying to identify with his feelings, needs, and emotions. For instance, in the evening when a patient tends to wander (a symptom called "sundowners"), teens can acknowledge the wandering and try to enter the patient's world, one in which Grandfather always came home from work in the evening, had supper with the family, and did outside chores. By picking up on that and talking to him about his chores, his family, his work day, a teenager thus helps him relax (Whyte). Holding hands, sitting beside him, and hugging are also important ways to say "I care." Communication problems diminish, then, with careful verbal and nonverbal cues.

Behavior problems, however, challenge the most tolerant families and teens. Emotional instability is one of the more common symptoms. Grandmother may yell or argue, getting easily upset seemingly overnothing (Powell 144). As one family member explained,

> The worst thing . . . is his temper. He used to be easygoing. Now he is always hollering over the least little thing. Last night he told our ten year old that Alaska is not a state. He was hollering and yelling and stalked out of the room. Then when I asked him to take a bath we had a real fight. He insisted he had already taken a bath (Mace 9).

Other verbal abuse may come when Grandmother accuses her family of stealing her jewelry. Grandfather may insult his grand-children by telling their friends, "They keep me prisoner in this house"; or he may direct rude remarks to their friends, like "You oughta get a haircut." Young people have difficulty dealing with this kind of socially unacceptable behavior.

The unacceptable behavior, however, is not always verbal. Teens hesitate to bring friends home because they may find Grandfather sitting on the porch reading the newspaper and wearing nothing but his hat. When Grandmother eats with the wrong utensils—or without utensils—teens may be repulsed. Grandfather may finally remember to dress but have his shirt buttoned wrong or have his sweater on backwards or inside out. When Grandfather answers the phone but fails to tell his granddaughter about the young man's call, a crisis results.

To respond to such behavior problems, teens can face a real challenge. First, they should remember that "our familiar world has become strange and perhaps threatening to the person with brain damage who cannot manage to react in an ordinary way to an ordinary situation" (Powell 159). If Grandmother shouts or is angry, one must forget reasoning and logic. She cannot reason. Trying to reason with her most often leads to an argument. Instead, family members can quietly divert attention by changing the subject, looking at old photographs, singing old songs. Even ignoring unwanted behavior works better than reacting to it (Cohen 161-162). One psychiatrist explained that families can better deal with outbursts by remembering that the "angry lashing out of a patient is displaced anger at the disease" (Untitled sidebar 14). Above all, teens need to make sure that friends understand that Grandfather's illness "affects his memory of good manners [and that] the parts of the brain that make [him] behave as [he] should are also damaged" (Mace 107, 185). In short, his behavior is not anything he can control. As a result, professional caregivers tend to think of behavioral problems not as problems but as symptoms of a need or emotion. "Then we enter their world, help them relax, and thus prevent the behavior from recurring" (Whyte). Teens, however, as well as other family members, often find it difficult to distance themselves from the patient and let go of their own emotions. "The closer you are to someone, the harder it is to validate their world" (Whyte).

As a result of the victim's inability to control his or her behavior, the family—including teens—must adapt. If Grandmother can no longer use a knife and fork, she may do better with finger foods (Kent 34). If Grandfather can no longer handle buttons and zippers, pull-on clothing may meet his needs. If Grandmother insists on sleeping with her sweater on, she is doing nothing harmful (Mace 22). An analogy helps explain:

> It would be foolish to insist that a one-armed man eat chicken in the conventional manner, using fork and knife. Equally foolish would be drawing the conclusion that he is totally incapable of eating chicken. . . . The humane approach would be to let him use his fingers or give him an adapted utensil that can be used with one hand—either way, accommodating his deficits while letting him make full use of his remaining ability. So, too, persons with Alzheimer's disease cannot be forced into using resources that

they do not have, but they can be directed toward using fully those resources that they do retain (Zgola 104).

As a teen struggles to learn to deal with the patient, he may need help with solutions. Perhaps only outsiders can really help a teen cope with the siblinglike rivalry that arises when he gives up his room, a vacation, or other material things because of a grandparent with AD (Ronch 55). Outsiders, too, can help a teen cope with the grief she feels when someone who always baked cookies for her or babysat for her is now so dramatically changed that the roles are reversed: the teen babysits the grandmother (Mace 153). Traditionally, the best help comes either from counselors or support groups.

Teens face the same range of emotions that others face: anger, shame, self-pity, guilt, anxiety, depression, and stress (Oliver v-vi). As a result, young people need to learn everything they can so they know what is going to happen. The knowledge helps them better handle the inevitable problems (Stolen Tomorrows). Young people also need to know that other teens complain about common problems living with AD victims: having no privacy because Grandfather wanders; having to be quiet because Grandmother gets excited; complaining about the way Grandfather eats or acts; having to assume much more responsibility at home; receiving less and less attention from parents who must spend more and more time taking care of Grandmother (Mace 186). Teachers, other relatives, counselors—any adult not too tired from caring for the AD victim—can help teens "who cannot understand what they interpret as a loss of interest or of love by a patient" (Cohen 214). Teens who do not get help often become "demanding and rebellious, or show violent outbursts, and generally misbehave at home and school" (Cohen 214); thus, seeking help is best for everyone—the AD patient, parents, and teens themselves.

Other teens may need help coping with personal fears. Some fear that AD is contagious (it is not) or fear they will inherit the dementing illness. While certain studies do link Alzheimer's disease to heredity (Majeski), the statistics suggest that only a very small percentage of cases suggest genetic factors. In fact, "there are several ways to get Alzheimer's: inherit one of at least four bad genes, have too little of several key brain chemicals, or at some point in life suffer damage to the tiny blood vessels that nourish the brain" ("Quietly Closing" 112). Other teens fear alienation by their friends because of a grandparent's odd, even bizarre, behavior. Some teens, however, find some comfort in the recognition that numerous celebrities have suffered from AD: actors Rita Hayworth, Edmund O'Brien, and Arthur O'Connell; essayist E.B. White; artist Norman Rockwell; mystery writer Ross McDonald; jazz saxophonist Charlie Barnet; and boxing champion Sugar Ray Robinson ("Celebrity Victims" 626). Other teens in support groups note, when they explain to their friends that Grandfather is sick, that most friends are "sympathetic and understanding once they know what [the] situation is" (ADRDA, Especially 5). Personal fears diminish with understanding.

Coping with a loved one's dementia demands every capability families can muster, but sometimes the teenager becomes the unseen victim, left to muddle through on his own. As Dr. Monica Blumenthal of the University of Pittsburgh School of Medicine said. "In many ways, dementia is like death. It is the death of the mind. Most family members who are close to the patient will go through some phase of mourning which is often more grievous than that produced by death itself, [while others call the disease] a funeral that never ends" (Leroux 4). One teenager wrote of her grandfather,

> I love you
> I hated you
> I laughed at you
> I laughed with you
> I sang with you
> I danced with you
> I talked with you
> I yelled at you
> I listened to you

Perkins 9

I ignored you
and now
I miss you (Honel 139).

Just like King Lear's daughter Cordelia, teenage family members must reach for understanding and empathy. They need to understand how to respond to the debilitating illness—its cognitive degeneration, communication impairment, and behavioral symptoms. In addition, however, they also need supportive sympathy, perhaps counseling, to help them through the never-ending funeral of their loved one.

Works Cited

The Alzheimer's Disease and Related Disorders Association, Inc.
Alzheimer's Disease: Especially for Teenagers. Chicago: ADRDA,
1987.

—.Alzheimer's Disease Statistics. Chicago: ADRDA, Aug. 1991.

—.Communicating with the Alzheimer Patient. Chicago: ADRDA,
1990.

"Celebrity Victims." The CO Researcher 24 July 1992: 626.

"Chronology." The CO Researcher 24 July 1992: 625.

Cohen, Donna. The Loss of Self: A Family Resource for the Care of
Alzheimer's Disease and Related Disorders. New York: Norton,
1986.

Heston, Leonard L. The Vanishing Mind: A Practical Guide to
Alzheimer's Disease and Other Dementias. New York: W. H.
Freeman, 1991.

Honel, Rosalie Walsh. Journey with Grandpa: Our Family Struggle
with Alzheimer's Disease. Baltimore: Johns Hopkins University
Press, 1988.

Kent, Don. "Creating a Home That Speaks Their Language." Aging
Magazine 363-364 (1992): 32-34.

Leroux, Charles. Coping and Caring: Living with Alzheimer's Disease.
Washington, D.C.: American Association of Retired Persons,
Health Advocacy Services Program Department, 1986.

Mace, Nancy L. The 36-Hour Day: A Family Guide to Caring for
Persons with Alzheimer's Disease, Related Dementing Illnesses,
and Memory Loss in Later Life. Baltimore: Johns Hopkins
University Press, 1981.

Majeski, Tom. "New Study Links Alzheimer's Disease to Heredity." St.
Paul (Minnesota) Pioneer Press-Dispatch 19 April 1991 (Located
in NewsBank [Microform], Health, Education and Aging, 1991,
32:E6, fiche).

Martinson, Ida M., Catherine Chesla, and Marylou Muwaswes. "Caregiving Demands of Patients with Alzheimer's Disease." Journal of Community Health Nursing October 1993: 225-232.

Oliver, Rose. Coping with Alzheimer's: A Caregiver's Emotional Survival Guide. New York: Dodd, Mead, 1987.

Powell, Lenore S. Alzheimer's Disease: A Guide for Families. Reading, Mass.: Addison-Wesley, 1983.

"Quietly Closing in on Alzheimer's." Business Week 3 May 1993: 112-113.

Ronch, Judah L. Alzheimer's Disease: A Practical Guide for Those Who Help Others. New York: Continuum, 1989.

Shakespeare, William. Shakespeare: Twenty-Three Plays and the Sonnets. Ed. Thomas Marc Parrott. Rev. ed. New York: Charles Scribner's Sons, 1953.

"Stages of Alzheimer's Disease." Aging Magazine 363-364 (1992): 16-17.

Stolen Tomorrows. Videotape. Dev. Lincoln General Hospital, Van Nuys, Calif. AIMS Media, 1988. 26 min.

Tanner, Fredericka, and Sharon Shaw. Caring: A Family Guide to Managing the Alzheimer's Patient at Home. New York: New York City Alzheimer's Resource Center, program of New York City Department for the Aging, 1985.

Untitled sidebar. Aging Magazine 363-364 (1992): 14.

Whyte, Vickie. Dir. Alzheimer's Unit, McCurdy Healthcare Center, Evansville, Ind. Personal interview. 12 Aug. 1994.

You Are Not Alone. Videotape. Retirement Research Foundation Video Collection on Aging. Park Ridge, Ill.: Retirement Research Foundation, 1984. 28 min.

Zgola, Jitka M. Doing Things: A Guide to Programming Organized Activities for Persons with Alzheimer's Disease and Related Disorders. Baltimore: Johns Hopkins University Press, 1987.

ANALYSIS OF THE MLA PARENTHETICAL STYLE SAMPLE

The paper illustrates many of the important principles that should be evident in a research paper. While you can make observations on your own about the approach the sample paper takes, note these specifics:

- The topic is interesting, timely, and narrowed appropriately for the length of the paper. While the subject of Alzheimer's disease receives book-length attention from many authors, this writer narrowed the topic to something meaningful to her: how teenagers cope with a grandparent who has the disease. Thus, many of her sources included only a chapter or scattered segments appropriate to her topic. To locate the specific information needed, she used the tables of contents and the indexes to avoid nonproductive reading.

- The paper employs both primary and secondary research. Alicia's primary research comes from an interview with an Alzheimer's-care specialist who founded the Alzheimer's wing of the nursing home where Alicia volunteered. The primary research enhances the paper.

- Quotations support the writer's ideas. The few long quotations offer insight into researchers' findings or other authors' observations. Shorter quotations are often only key words or phrases. Notice, too, how these short quoted passages blend smoothly into the text, in some cases woven directly into the beginning, middle, or end of the writer's own sentences.

- Far more paraphrases appear than do quotations. The writer avoids a paper that is little more than a string of quotations. Because of her paraphrasing, the paper reads evenly and reflects a thoughtful analysis of relationships among ideas.

- The paragraphs are clearly organized. The paper includes a two-paragraph introduction (not part of the outline), and each of the remaining paragraphs corresponds to a main heading or subheading in the outline.

- Each paragraph demonstrates careful development. Numerous details—paraphrased or quoted—give the reader a variety of examples by which to clarify his/her understanding of the paragraph's topic.

- Paragraphs maintain unity. All paragraph details explain or otherwise elaborate upon the topic sentence. Extraneous details were deleted during the revision process.

- The paper exhibits good sentence variety and sophisticated writing technique. Short sentences create emphasis, especially when placed after lengthy sentences.

- Transitional words, phrases, and sentences move the reader smoothly from idea to idea and from paragraph to paragraph.

- The format, with accurate parenthetical notes and a list of works cited, follows the guidelines for good typing technique. Long quotations are set apart from the rest of the text. The bibliography page is accurate and complete, citing only those sources used in the text.

By following carefully all the steps in the research process, you will be able to develop a satisfactory research paper. Remember, however, that the particular form you follow will probably be determined by your teacher or by department or school policy. As a result, in order to model as many alternate forms as possible, we have included four additional formats. Among all of the models, therefore, you should find an example of virtually anything you need.

Best wishes!

SAMPLE MLA ENDNOTE STYLE PAPER

The following excerpt from the complete paper above illustrates another widely accepted style, the MLA endnote style. The documentation appears in the text only as raised numbers. The numbers in turn refer to a list of notes at the end of the paper. The *bibliography* list for an endnote style paper follows the *endnote page(s)* and is prepared exactly the same as the list of works cited for the parenthetical style paper.

Alicia Perkins
Ms. R. O. Cooper
Senior English
14 January 20—

When Alzheimer's Hits Home

As a reflection of the human condition, early literature includes references to "old timer's" disease. Perhaps Shakespeare's King Lear best defines the malady when he says to his daughter Cordelia and her husband:

I fear I am not in my perfect mind.
Methinks I should know you, and know this man;
Yet I am doubtful; for I am mainly ignorant
What place this is; and all the skill I have
Remembers not these garments; nor I know not
Where I did lodge last night. Do not laugh at me.[1]

Lear no doubt suffers from irreversible brain deterioration known today as Alzheimer's disease, or AD. Unnamed until 1906 when Alois Alzheimer described the condition,[2] AD, an organic disease that destroys brain cells, now affects up to four million Americans.[3] Within fifty years, predictions say that fourteen million sufferers will face the fourth leading cause of death in America.[4]

When a relative has AD, however, statistics, frightening or not, take a back seat. The disease referred to as the "dementing thief of minds and destroyer of personalities"[5] so dramatically changes a loved one that families struggle to cope; and among family members, young people face unique problems. In the midst of striving to understand their own changing adolescent roles, they find themselves also striving to understand a changing grandparent. They face a tough challenge both to understand and to deal with the grandparent's cognitive deterioration, communication impairments, and behavior modifications.

Any form of dementia, AD being the worst, involves the "loss or impairment of mental powers."[6] The impairment begins slowly, almost imperceptibly: forgetting names, words, and later, meals; being unable to make change, balance a checkbook, or learn anything new; getting lost; forgetting the day or month. As the disease progresses, victims lose the ability to track time, even confusing day and night. As a result, they may want to dress at odd hours, want to leave as soon as they arrive somewhere, think they have been left alone for days or weeks when it is only for a few minutes.[7] "For the person with a memory impairment, life may be like constantly coming into the middle of a movie: one has no idea what happened just before what is happening now."[8] The loss of cognitive powers may best be exemplified this way:

> Mary gradually lost the ability to make sense out of what her eyes and ears told her. Noises and . . .

Perkins 3

Notes

[1] William Shakespeare, <u>Shakespeare: Twenty-Three Plays and the Sonnets</u>, ed. Thomas Marc Parrott, rev. ed. (New York: Charles Scribner's Sons, 1953) 814.

[2] "Chronology," <u>The CO Researcher</u> 24 July 1992: 625.

[3] <u>You Are Not Alone</u>, videotape, Retirement Research Foundation Video Collection on Aging, Park Ridge, Ill., Retirement Research Foundation, 1984.

[4] The Alzheimer's Disease and Related Disorders Association, Inc., <u>Alzheimer's Disease Statistics</u> (Chicago: ADRDA, Aug. 1991) I.

[5] Charles Leroux, <u>Coping and Caring: Living with Alzheimer's Disease</u> (Washington, D. C.: American Association of Retired Persons, Health Advocacy Services Program Department, 1986) 2.

[6] Nancy L. Mace, <u>The 36-Hour Day: A Family Guide to Caring for Persons with Alzheimer's Disease, Related Dementing Illnesses, and Memory Loss in Later Life</u> (Baltimore: Johns Hopkins University Press, 1981) 5.

[7] "Stages of Alzheimer's Disease," <u>Aging Magazine</u> 364 (1992): 16-17.

[8] Mace 24.

Note: The Works Cited page is the same for endnote style as that for the parenthetical style paper.

SAMPLE MLA FOOTNOTE STYLE PAPER

The footnote style that follows is still preferred by some. Although exceedingly difficult to develop on most computers, this format was originally set forth by MLA as most suitable for general purposes. It is no longer so highly favored but it still has its advocates.

This excerpted model also illustrates the use of *a cover or title page* and an *outline page*.

When Alzheimer's Hits Home

Alicia Perkins

English 101

Dr. Elizabeth K. Swenson

December 10, 20—

When Alzheimer's Hits Home

Thesis sentence: Teenagers face a tough challenge both to understand and to deal with a loved one afflicted with Alzheimer's disease as he or she regresses through cognitive deterioration, communication impairments, and behavior problems.

I.   Understanding the patient's cognitive problems
    A. Typical characteristics
        1. Defining the regression
        2. Describing the effects
    B. Suitable responses

II. Understanding the patient's communication impairment
    A. Typical characteristics
    B. Suitable responses

III. Understanding the patient's behavior problems
    A. Typical characteristics
        1. Verbal
        2. Physical
    B. Suitable responses
        1. Understanding
        2. Adaptation

IV. Getting additional help
    A. To understand the patient
    B. To address personal fears

i

When Alzheimer's Hits Home

As a reflection of the human condition, early literature includes references to "old timer's" disease. Perhaps Shakespeare's King Lear best defines the malady when he says to his daughter Cordelia and her husband:

I fear I am not in my perfect mind.
Methinks I should know you, and know this man;
Yet I am doubtful; for I am mainly ignorant
What place this is; and all the skill I have
Remembers not these garments; nor I know not
Where I did lodge last night. Do not laugh at me.[1]

Lear no doubt suffers from irreversible brain deterioration known today as Alzheimer's disease, or AD. Unnamed until 1906 when Alois Alzheimer described the condition,[2] AD, an organic disease that destroys brain cells, now affects up to four million Americans.[3] Within fifty years, predictions say that fourteen million sufferers will face the fourth leading cause of death in America.[4]

When a relative has AD, however, statistics, frightening or not, take a back seat. The disease referred to as the "dementing thief of minds and destroyer of personalities"[5] so dramatically changes a loved one that families struggle to cope; and among family members.

---

[1] William Shakespeare, Shakespeare: Twenty-Three Plays and the Sonnets, ed. Thomas Marc Parrott, rev. ed. (New York: Charles Scribner's Sons, 1953) 814.

[2] "Chronology," The CO Researcher 24 July 1992: 625.

[3] You Are Not Alone, videotape, Retirement Research Foundation Video Collection on Aging, Park Ridge, Ill., Retirement Research Foundation, 1984.

[4] The Alzheimer's Disease and Related Disorders Association, Inc., Alzheimer's Disease Statistics (Chicago: ADRDA, Aug. 1991) I.

[5] Charles Leroux, Coping and Caring: Living with Alzheimer's Disease (Washington, D. C.: American Association of Retired PerPersons PersonsPersons, Health Advocacy Services Program Department, 1986).

SAMPLE APA STYLE PAPER

The *Publication Manual of the American Psychological Association* establishes a specific style for psychology papers. In addition, however, some high schools, colleges, and universities require the style for all research papers. Referred to as the APA style, it calls for a distinctive form. Note especially that the title page includes only three items: the title (in twelve to fifteen words), the student's name, and the student's school affiliation.

Note these particulars about the title page:

- All three items should be double-spaced, centered left to right and top to bottom.
- A title requiring more than one line is also double spaced.
- A running head, which is a shortened version of the title, appears at the top right margin, 1-1/2" from the top and right edges.
- Page number (1) appears a double space below the running head and flush with the right margin.
- Running head is repeated, centered, at the bottom of the title page.

An abstract follows, summarizing the paper. Follow these details for preparing the abstract page:

- The abstract page includes the same running head and page numbering as does the title page.
- The title, *Abstract*, appears centered a double space below the page number.
- The text begins a double space below the title.
- The abstract is a single paragraph written in block form (i.e., without the usual paragraph indentation).
- The abstract should be 75 to 100 words for theoretical articles or reviews and 100 to 150 words for empirical papers.

The body of the paper follows these formatting details:

- All pages maintain 1-1/2" margins all around.
- All pages have a running head with the sequential page numbers a double space below, flush with the right margin.
- The entire paper is double-spaced with a few exceptions:
- When readability is enhanced, such as in tables and figure citations, single spacing is permitted.
- When readability is enhanced, such as before major subheadings, before footnotes,

and before and after tables in the text, triple- or quadruple-spacing is permitted.
- The first page of the paper repeats the title, centered, a double space below the page number.
- Text begins a double space below the title.
- All paragraphs are indented five spaces.
- The introduction, which is unlabeled, explains the problem the research has examined.
- All other parts of the paper are labeled. Common labels include *Method*, *Results*, *Discussion*, and *References*. These can be considered separate chapters.
- Each new part or new chapter begins on a new page.
- The top margins on these new pages may be wider than on other pages, usually, however, no more than two inches.
- Headings of the same level are typed in the same format, i.e., in all capital letters, underscored, or indented.

The documentary notes are parenthetical. They follow these details:

- The author's last name is followed by a comma and the date of publication.

When the author's name appears in the text, only the date appears in parentheses.

If reference is made to a specific page or chapter, or if a quotation is included, the parenthetical note must also include a page or chapter number.

- Use the abbreviation *p.* or *pp.* preceding page numbers.

Compare these examples:
    (Smith, 1992)
    (Smith, 1992, p. 78)
    (Smith, 1992, pp. 78-81)

- If notes refer to a publication without author credit, use the title and date of publication. Omit quotation marks around such titles, but do italicize (underline) any such titles if they are italicized (underlined) in the reference list.

Any charts, tables, or figures are incorporated at the appropriate point in the text.

- Short tables may appear on a page with some text.
- A longer chart or figure appears on a separate page, inserted immediately after the page on which it is first mentioned.
- Put titles and labels at the top for tables and at the bottom for figures.

Instead of a bibliography, the APA style calls for a reference list.

- The reference list must include every citation in the text.
- The form for entries differs considerably from the MLA style. Check these details:

> The surnames are accompanied not by first names but only by initials. When there is more than one author or editor, all names are inverted (last name first followed by initials).
>
> Parentheses are used around the date of publication.
>
> Capital letters are omitted in all but the first word and proper names of article and book titles.
>
> Quotation marks are omitted around article titles.
>
> Initial capital letters are used for titles of professional journals.
>
> Volume numbers of periodicals are underscored.

- Entries are double-spaced with hanging indentation, the second line and following lines being indented only three spaces, rather than five as in the MLA style.

Any appendices providing statistical data are placed after the references page.

- Each appendix begins on a new page.
- The running head and consecutive page numbering continues through the appendices.
- Titles, like "Appendix A," are centered a double-space below the page number.

The model on the following pages illustrates many of the essential formatting details of the APA style.

When Alzheimer's Disease Hits Home: Responding to Patient
Regression and the Family's Resulting Emotions

Alicia Perkins

Mt. Vernon Junior College

Abstract

Teenagers, often the unseen victim in a family's battle with Alzheimer's disease (AD), must learn to cope with the anger, frustration, and depression—their own and that of others—brought on by the mentally debilitating disease. Teens struggling to find their own emerging adult personalities struggle further to find the patience to deal with grandparents whose problems of cognitive deterioration, communication impairments, and behavior modifications leave everyone exhausted. Sometimes outside sources like counseling and support groups provide the necessary help for young people to avoid the rebelliousness and other negative behaviors that they sometimes display in reaction to the ripple effect of the grandparent's illness.

When Alzheimer's Disease Hits Home: Responding to Patient Regression and the Family's Resulting Emotion

As a reflection of the human condition, early literature includes references to "old timer's" disease. Perhaps Shakespeare's King Lear best defined the malady when he said to his daughter Cordelia and her husband:

I fear I am not in my perfect mind.
Methinks I should know you, and know this man;
Yet I am doubtful; for I am mainly ignorant
What place this is; and all the skill I have
Remembers not these garments; nor I know not
Where I did lodge last night. Do not laugh at me.
(4.7.63-68)

Lear suffers from irreversible brain deterioration known today as Alzheimer's disease, or AD. Unnamed until 1906 when Alois Alzheimer described the condition at a meeting of the South German Society of Neurologists (Chronology, 1992), AD, an organic disease that destroys brain cells, now affects up to four million Americans (You Are Not Alone, 1984). Within fifty years, fourteen million sufferers will face the fourth leading cause of death in America (ADRDA, AD Statistics, 1991).

When a relative has AD, however, statistics, frightening or not, take a back seat. The disease referred to as the "dementing thief of minds and destroyer of personalities" (Leroux, 1986, p. 2) so dramatically changes a loved one that families struggle to cope; and among family members, young people face unique problems. In the midst of striving to understand their own changing adolescent roles, they find themselves also striving to understand a changing grandparent. They face the grandparent's cognitive deterioration, communication impairments, and behavior problems, struggling to find solutions to each of the problems.

Any form of dementia, AD being the worst, involves the "loss or impairment of mental powers" (Mace, 1981, p. 5). The impairment begins slowly, almost imperceptibly: forgetting names, words, and later, meals; being unable to make change, balance a checkbook, or learn anything new; getting lost; forgetting the day or month. As the disease progresses, victims lose track of time, even confusing day and night. As a result, they may want to dress at odd hours, want to leave as soon as they arrive somewhere, think they have been left alone for days or weeks when it is only for a few minutes (Stages of AD, 1992). "For the person with a memory impairment, life may be like constantly coming into the middle of a movie: one has no idea what happened just before what is happening now" (Mace, 1981, p. 24). The loss of cognitive powers may best be exemplified this way:

> Mary gradually lost the ability to make sense out of what her eyes and ears told her. Noises and confusion made her feel panicky. She couldn't understand, they couldn't explain . . . .

References

The Alzheimer's Disease and Related Disorders Association, Inc. Alzheimer's disease statistics. (1991). Chicago: ADRDA

Chronology. (1992). The CQ Researcher. 2, 614-640.

Cohen, D. (1986). The loss of self: A family resource for the care of Alzheimer's disease and related disorders. New York: Norton.

Leroux, C. (1986). Coping and caring: Living with Alzheimer's disease. Washington, D. C.: American Association of Retired Persons, Health Advocacy Services Program Department.

Mace, N. L. (1981). The 36-hour day: A family guide to caring for persons with Alzheimer's disease, related dementing illnesses, and memory loss in later life. Baltimore: Johns Hopkins University Press.

Martinson, I. M., Chesla, C., and Muwaswes, M. (1993). Caregiving demands of patients with Alzheimer's disease. Journal of Community Health Nursing. 10, 225-232.

Quietly closing in on Alzheimer's. (1993). Business Week. 112-113.

Stages of Alzheimer's disease. (1992). Aging Magazine. 363-364, 16-17.

You are not alone. (1984). Videotape. Retirement Research Foundation Video Collection on Aging. Park Ridge, Ill.: Retirement Research Foundation.

SAMPLE NUMBERED BIBLIOGRAPHY STYLE PAPER

The numbered bibliography style simplifies documentation. Some readers object to this style because they must flip to the bibliography to determine each source as it appears in the text. Other readers, especially those who place less emphasis on sources, prefer its uncluttered format. Writers generally like it because it eases documentation. Here's how the numbered bibliography style works.

Before writing the final draft of the paper, prepare an alphabetical listing of sources used in the paper. Number the list consecutively, beginning with 1. (Note that other arrangements are also possible. For instance, scientific papers often list the sources in the order in which they are first cited in the text. Use whichever arrangement works best for your purposes.)

When you document a source in your text, refer parenthetically to the work by number. Follow the number with a comma and space, and then add the page number. A numbered parenthetical note looks like this: (8, 32). In this case, 8 refers to the eighth source listed in the numbered bibliography, and *32* refers to the page number within the source. A multiple-page reference looks like this: (12, 114-123).

The following excerpt illustrates the numbered bibliography style:

When Alzheimer's Hits Home

As a reflection of the human condition, early literature includes references to "old timer's" disease. Even Shakespeare's King Lear no doubt suffers from the irreversible brain deterioration known today as Alzheimer's disease, or AD. Unnamed until 1906 when Alois Alzheimer described the condition (2, 625), AD, an organic disease that destroys brain cells, now affects up to four million Americans (6). Within fifty years, predictions say that fourteen million sufferers will face the fourth leading cause of death in America (1, 1).

When a relative has AD, however, statistics, frightening or not, take a back seat. The disease referred to as the "dementing thief of minds and destroyer of personalities" (3, 2) so dramatically changes a loved one that families struggle to cope; and among family members, young people face unique problems. In the midst of striving to understand their own changing adolescent roles, they may also find themselves striving to understand a changing grandparent. They face a tough challenge both to understand and to deal with the grandparent's cognitive deterioration, communication impairments, and behavior modifications. . . .

Works Cited

1. The Alzheimer's Disease and Related Disorders Association, Inc., <u>Alzheimer's Disease Statistics</u>. Chicago: ADRDA, Aug. 1991.
2. "Chronology." <u>The CQ Researcher</u> 24 July 1992: 625.
3. Leroux, Charles. <u>Coping and Caring: Living with Alzheimer's Disease</u>. Washington, D. C.: American Association of Retired Persons, Health Advocacy Services Program Department, 1986.
4. Shakespeare, William. <u>Shakespeare: Twenty-Three Plays and the Sonnets</u>. Ed. Thomas Marc Parrott. Rev. ed. New York: Charles Scribner's Sons, 1953.
5. Tanner, Fredericka, and Sharon Shaw. <u>Caring: A Family Guide to Managing the Alzheimer's Patient at Home</u>. New York: New York City Alzheimer's Resource Center, program of New York City Department for the Aging, 1985.
6. <u>You Are Not Alone</u>. Videotape. Retirement Research Foundation Video Collection on Aging. Park Ridge, Ill.: Retirement Research Foundation, 1984.

NOTES

NOTES

NOTES

NOTES

NOTES

NOTES

NOTES

NOTES

NOTES

NOTES

NOTES

NOTES

NOTES

NOTES

NOTES

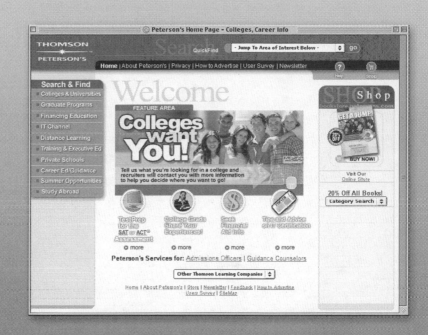